THE NUTS AND BOLTS OF CHURCH GROWTH

Paul W. Powell

BROADMAN PRESS
Nashville, Tennessee

© Copyright 1982 • Broadman Press
All rights reserved.
4225-42
ISBN: 0-8054-2542-x
Dewey Decimal Classification: 254.5
Subject Heading: CHURCH GROWTH
Library of Congress Catalog Card Number: 81-68926
Printed in the United States of America

Introduction

Your church can grow! I really believe that. What's more, the Lord wants it to grow. He earnestly wants lost people to be found and brought into his family as disciples and responsible church members.

How could our Lord feel otherwise? The greatest evidence for the living Lord is always a living, loving, laughing, and lifting church. The church is the body of Christ. How can we show that Christ is alive if his body, the church, is dead?

One problem we face is that many churches are settling for less than our Lord would—a full house (Luke 14:23). Church houses are half empty and church members are fully satisfied. Empty seats do not honor God. Vacant pews do not recommend him to an indifferent and preoccupied world. But a full house is always a different story. If God's people would just show up, our churches would fill up, and the world would sit up and take notice.

The purpose of this book is to encourage you and give you practical help toward that end. This book is about the nuts and bolts of church growth. It is not a book of theory. The things I have written have worked and are working right now to help our church to grow. Moreover, some of these things will work to produce growth where you are. They will work if you will work. If this book accomplishes that, it will be well worth the work that went into it.

I am especially grateful to my faithful secretary, Gloria Ortega, for typing and retyping the manuscript, to Gerrie Milburn for editing it, and to my great staff and church for giving me the time and the inspiration to write it.

Contents

1
What God Has Done

I read a quip recently that said, "Let him who often toots his own horn take heed lest he run his battery down." That's a loose translation of the proverb that says, "Don't praise yourself; let others do it!" (Prov. 27:2, TLB).

What I have written here is not intended to be a boast about Green Acres Baptist Church. It is intended to give a boost to you. During the past eight years, our church has enjoyed a marvelous growth. I am often asked to share in conferences and at banquets some of what has happened in our church and why it has happened. What I have written here is an effort to share in writing those things that I am so often asked to share in person.

Some churches start out with a fever and end up with a chill. Their growth shoots up like a rocket and comes down like a rock. The history of Green Acres Baptist Church in Tyler, Texas, has been one of steady and significant growth. Our church was born well. It began as a mission twenty-five years ago, and it was self-supporting from the first Sunday the people met in their new building. Within a year, it became an independent church.

During the past eight years, Green Acres has been among the leading churches in Texas in baptisms, Sunday School growth, and missions support. The only churches that have consistently exceeded us in these categories have been in the large, metropolitan areas. Tyler is an East Texas community of 70,720 people. It has grown 22.4 percent, from 57,770 to 70,720 in the last ten years.

During this same period of time, our church membership has grown 141 percent, our average Sunday School attendance has increased 154 percent. Our total gifts have increased 589 percent.

The Infusion of New Life

A church is healthiest when there is a continual infusion of new life in it. New people keep a church from spiritual stagnation. They bring new ideas, new energy, and new enthusiasm into the fellowship. In the past six years, we have averaged over 520 additions per year, or ten per Sunday. We have now grown to a current membership of 4,300 people.

Fizz or Fizzle

Thirty-five percent of these new members have come into our fellowship by baptism. That's important to us. Evangelism is to the church what CO^2 is to a carbonated drink. Without evangelism, there is no spiritual fizz in the church. A church without the fizz of evangelism will soon fizzle out. In the past seven years, we have baptized an average of 157 people per year.

We work at keeping evangelism central in all that we do. When I came as the pastor eight years ago, I told the people that our goal was to build the greatest evangelistic church in East Texas. The word *greatest* is not to suggest the idea of a competitive spirit. We are not out to beat anybody else. It is used only with reference to our potential. I believe the potential of our church is the greatest in our area, so we must measure up to it.

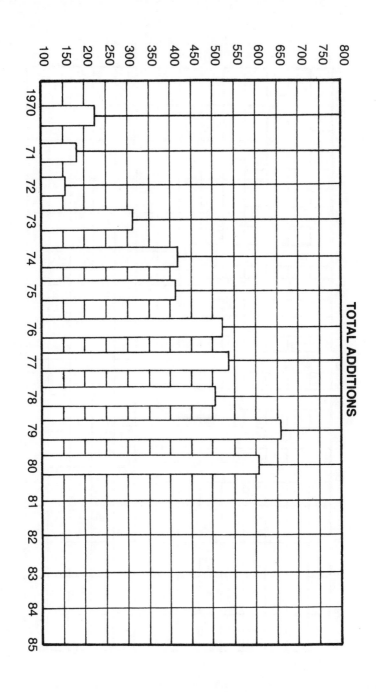

TOTAL ADDITIONS

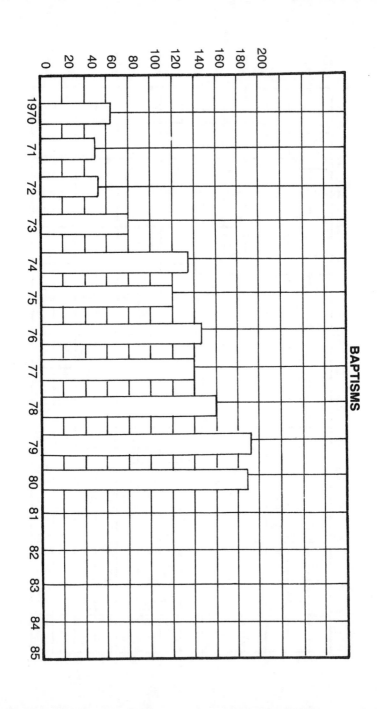

BAPTISMS

Numbers Count and We Count Numbers

I am unapologetically numbers conscious. Numbers count with us, and we count numbers. Have you noticed that those who minimize numbers usually do not have any to emphasize? Numbers count with the government, and so they take a census every ten years. Numbers count with the Chamber of Commerce, and so they post the population of their community on the city limits sign. Numbers count at athletic contests, and so the announcer usually tells you not only the number present at the contest but also the number of no-shows. Numbers count with universities, and so they proudly advertise any increase in enrollment.

I am on the board of directors of a local bank. In our monthly directors' meeting, we always receive a report on the number of new accounts opened and the number of accounts closed. We think numbers are important. They are an indication of growth and progress. They are not the only measure, but they are one measure.

Quantity *Versus* Quality

But some people think that churches should be different. They think we shouldn't be concerned about numbers.

They believe we should emphasize quality, not quantity. They feel we should place priority on discipleship, not evangelism. But any discipleship that falls short of evangelism is a shallow and an incomplete discipleship. Any discipler who does not witness and evangelize does not understand enough about discipleship to be a teacher.

Jesus didn't say, "Follow me, and I'll make you an expert Bible teacher." He didn't say, "Follow me, and I'll give you a deeper life." He didn't say, "Follow me, and I'll teach you how to memorize Scripture." He said, "Follow me and I will make you become fishers of men" (Mark

1:17, RSV). Bible study, a deeper life, and Scripture memorization prepare us to be the best fishers of men, but they are never an end in themselves.

Incidentally, an evangelism that does not go on to discipleship is a shallow and incomplete evangelism. The two are not competitors. They are companions.

One is a number. Numbers represent people. We don't count chairs or hymnals—only people. To say that numbers don't count is to say that people don't count.

God is apparently interested in numbers also. There is a whole book in the Bible called Numbers. When Jesus fed the multitudes, somebody counted the crowd; then the Holy Spirit led the Gospel writers to record that number for us. The fact we are told that five thousand people were fed helps us to see the magnitude of the miracle.

Jesus didn't feed just a Sunday School class. He didn't just cater a small wedding reception. He fed a whole town—five thousand in all. What a miracle!

The number of converts at Pentecost were counted and recorded. The Book of Acts is full of words like *multiplied, added,* and *great numbers.* Why, then, shouldn't numbers count with us also?

The Real Strength

The real strength of a church is in its Sunday School. It is in the small class on an age-group basis that discipleship takes place and a caring and sharing fellowship is established. When church growth is built on the strength of the preacher's personality alone, it will not be lasting. When the pastor moves on, attendance will drop off. We have tried to avoid that in our church. We have majored on building a strong, Bible-centered Sunday School so that no matter who is in the pulpit the church will continue to prosper and

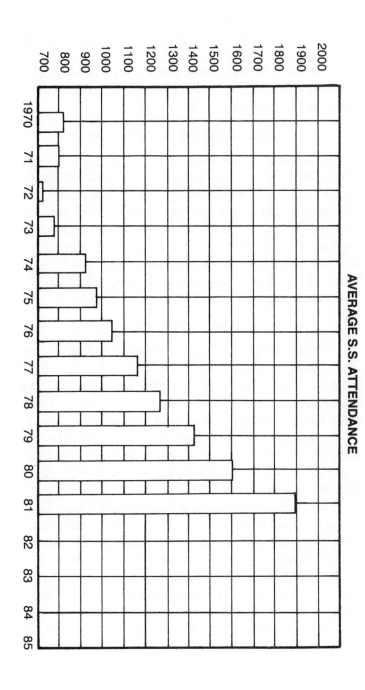

AVERAGE S.S. ATTENDANCE

grow. In the past eight years, our average Sunday School attendance has grown from 711 to 1,807. That is an increase of 154 percent.

Growing Bigger and Stronger

When people love the Lord's church and are happy with its program, they will give generously and joyfully. Our growth in the area of stewardship has been faster than any other area of church life. We have increased 589 percent in the last eight years. This is due not only to an increase in the number of people we have but also to the depth of their commitment. We have grown stronger as we have grown larger. Our gifts have increased from $300,000 to $2,000,000 per year in the last eight years.

The Rest of the Story

These statistics, however, tell only the part of the story. Our church also maintains a missionary home which is made available to furloughing missionaries free of charge. We operate a foster home, have our own retreat center, and a family recreation center on a nearby lake.

In the past eight years, we have built six buildings for ourselves, purchased ten houses and lots adjacent to our church, and either built or helped to build ten mission churches at home and abroad.

Five years ago we built our Family Life Center which is one of the finest church recreation buildings in our nation. It contains a full-sized gymnasium, a running track, two racquetball courts, a game room, six bowling lanes, a snack bar, a weight lifting and exercise room, saunas and whirlpools, a crafts room, a children's game room, a prayer chapel, den, and a commercial kitchen.

This building was followed by one of the finest chil-

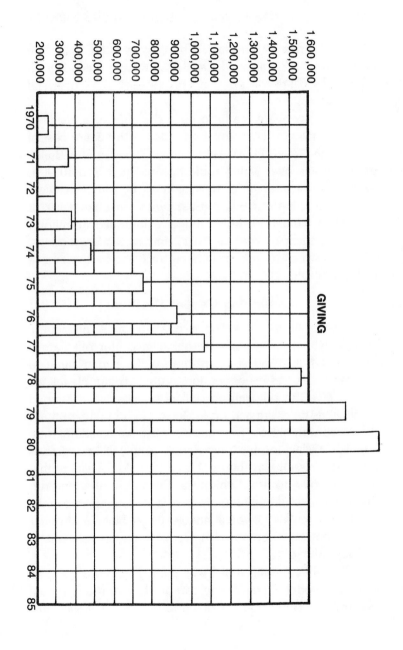

GIVING

dren's buildings in our state. The cost of our Family Life Center was 1.2 million dollars. Our people pledged 600 thousand dollars toward that building and then overpaid their pledges.

When we were ready to build the children's building, we asked the church members to pledge the entire cost of the building—$900,000. When this "Together We Build" program was over, our people had pledged $1,240,000. While we were building the children's building, we were also constructing our own retreat center on Lake Tyler. It includes a beautiful lakeside lodge, a forty-bed dormitory, two private cabins, nature trails, and recreation facilities. The retreat center was completely paid for by the time it was completed.

Launching Gospel Missiles

Green Acres has always been a great missionary church. So, when plans were being made for our Family Life Center, we had some resistance. One man came to visit me to express his opposition to the building. He felt we should give the one million dollars to missions. I listened carefully as he expressed his feelings. Then I told him that I disagreed with him for two reasons. First, we could not raise a million dollars for missions. People simply will not give as much for missions as they will give to build a building that they are going to use themselves. Second, in the long run the building would mean more than a million dollars to missions. The building would enable us to build a stronger church that could be an even greater force for missions in the days ahead.

Time has proven that I was right. If you are going to launch a model airplane, you can do that from any school playground. But if you are going to launch a ballistics missile, you must have a strong launching pad. We are in the business of launching gospel missiles around the world and must build a strong base to do that effectively.

Four years ago we set our Christmas foreign mission offering goal at 20 thousand dollars. However, our missions committee had learned of the need for a church building in the small border city of Diaz Ordaz, Mexico. The cost of the building was estimated to be 20 thousand dollars. So, we challenged our people to give 40 thousand dollars instead of 20 thousand dollars for foreign missions so we could build that church. The response was so great that within three weeks the 40 thousand dollars had been given.

Before the church in Mexico was actually completed, it had cost us 35 thousand dollars, but all the money was available when it was needed. We have maintained a continued ministry in that city ever since.

Groups from our church have made over sixteen mission trips at home and abroad during the past eight years. These have resulted in scores of smaller mission undertakings, such as providing an organ for a seminary in Belém, Brazil; paying for a television ministry in Pôrto Velho, Brazil; and supporting many local pastors and seminary students around the world.

Most recently we have undertaken to evangelize the country of Belize (formerly British Honduras) in Central America. In the next five years, we plan to build twenty church buildings, distribute between twenty-five and thirty thousand copies of the Scriptures, and train the national pastors.

God's Timing Is Perfect

The response to this mission project has been overwhelming. The first need, according to our missionary, Otis

Brady, was to purchase a five-acre farm that would be used as a training and retreat center for nationals and a base of operation for visiting missionary teams. The cost of the farm was 25 thousand dollars. I had in mind a man I wanted to ask to give the money for this project. Three days after I returned home from Belize, I was having breakfast in a local restaurant, when who should walk in but the very man I wanted to see. I shared with him briefly what was on my heart, and we made an appointment for a longer visit at a later time. Because of conflicting schedules, we made and broke three different dinner engagements before we finally got together. This didn't bother me because there was no apparent hurry. When we did meet, I shared my desires and dreams with him more extensively. He said, "Give me a few days to think about it. I will let you know something by Sunday."

The next Sunday I passed him in the hall. He said, "I have thought it over, and I will give the 25 thousand dollars for the farm."

The next day we called our missionary in Belize to tell him the news. He responded, "Thank the Lord! The man who was selling the farm had promised to hold it for us only until today. We had to let him know what we intended to do by tonight or he was going to sell the farm to someone else."

No one had told me that before. I wasn't even aware that we were working on a deadline. When I heard this, I thought to myself, *God's timing is always perfect. He is never early and he is never late. He is always right on time.*

The Best Is Yet to Come

I hope you don't get the idea that this has all been a bed of roses. Roses, even in Tyler, the rose capital of the world, have thorns. Achievement in all of these areas has come by blood, sweat, and tears.

And we are not through yet. At this very moment we are struggling over whether to launch into a 3 million dollar, two-building project or to go to three worship services and two Sunday Schools. We are praying earnestly for God's leadership concerning the future of our church.

I have learned that there are only two kinds of pain a church experiences. There is growing pain, and there is dying pain. Neither is very enjoyable, but I surely prefer the growing pains to any other alternative.

Now, what about the future? I am optimistic! I feel like composer Darius Milhaud, who has written well over four hundred works. He was once asked, "If you had to go to desert island, which of your compositions would you take with you?"

"I'd take some blank paper," he replied. "My favorite composition is always the one I will write tomorrow."

I feel the same way about our church. The most important part of our story is not that which you have just read. It is the part that we are writing today and that which we will write tomorrow.

2
Roadblocks to Growth

The first step to building a growing church is to make a commitment to growth. That being so, there are two basic questions every church needs to answer. Do you want to grow? If the answer is yes, then the second question is, What methods will we use to grow?

There was a time when I thought that all churches wanted to grow. I grew up in a church that was alive, evangelistic, and growing. I thought that all churches were that way. Then one night, early in my ministry, I was discussing the possibility of a new building with a long-range plans committee of my church. I said to the group, "Men, if we are going to grow, we must build this building." The chairman of the committee looked at me and said in a matter-of-fact way, "Who said we wanted to grow?"

For the first time, I realized that not all churches are interested in growth. There are many reasons for this.

More Afraid of Life Than Death

Some churches do not want to grow because of their lack of faith. Growth is risky. It usually involves new programs, new staff people, and new buildings. New things scare us, especially those that involve new debts.

Invariably, the first question asked when a new proposal is made is, How much will it cost? That, of course, ought to be the last question asked. The first question ought to be, Does God want us to do it? or Do we need it?

The work of God has always been associated with poverty. I do not know of a growing church anywhere that has all the money that it needs in advance. The people decide what they believe God wants them to do, and they trust him to supply all of their needs "according to his riches in glory by Christ Jesus" (Phil. 4:19).

But fear of the unknown and the unforeseeable future causes many churches and preachers to choose the security of mediocrity or even stagnation over the risk of growth and progress.

Let me illustrate. In every church I have pastored full time over the last twenty-five years, we have either built a building or started a building program. In my first pastorate, we built a new parsonage and a new educational building. In my second, we built a Mexican mission. In my third, we drew plans and secured pledges for a recreation building. In my present pastorate, we have built two major buildings on our church site and four buildings at our retreat center. But I have never proposed a building program but that someone raised questions about the stability of the economy.

The future is always uncertain. We can never be sure of the economy. So, building and growth must always involve an element of risk. Many churches simply do not have the courage or the faith to venture out.

This is especially true of churches filled with older members. That puzzles me. The older a Christian grows and the longer he has walked with God, the greater his faith ought to be. The most optimistic, progressive, and daring people on earth ought to be elderly saints who have seen God do his mighty work over their lifetimes. But, alas, it is not so. Even the people of God seem to grow more conservative and less adventurous with the passing years.

John A. Shedd said, "A ship in the harbor is safe—but that is not what ships are for." We all know that ships are for sailing and carrying cargo, but it is always risky business to head out for the open seas.

The captain and the crew that are afraid of stormy seas or getting salt spray in their eyes will never go anywhere. The problem with many churches today is that they have forgotten what they are for and they are playing it safe in the harbor.

A ship in the harbor is safe from storms, but it is not safe from dry rot.

James Byrnes, former secretary of state, summed up the attitude of many when he said, "Too many people think security instead of opportunity. They seem to be more afraid of life than death."

Who Said Big Was Bad?

Some churches do not want to grow because they mistakenly equate smallness with spirituality. They believe that big is bad in churches. Several years ago when we were raising money for a new building, I chanced to meet one of our men in the Dallas-Fort Worth Airport. I told him that I would like to get together with him and discuss the proposed new building. He told me that he would be glad to meet with me, but he had serious reservations about the entire building program. A few days later we got together for lunch. I started the conversation by asking him to make a sacrificial pledge to the building. He laughed and said, "If I did that I would have to give the whole building." He wasn't kidding. Then he went on to say, "I'm not sure I'm for that building anyhow. I don't like big churches. Big churches tend to become liberal and to lose their effectiveness. They cease to have that personal touch."

He didn't like big government. He didn't like big cities. So, naturally he didn't like big churches. The only big thing he seemed to believe in was his own business. It was OK if that grew bigger and bigger.

There are a lot of people who share that feeling. Where do we get the idea that small is more spiritual than big? If a church is small because its people do not visit or pray, if a church is small because its people are not missionary-minded, if a church is small because its people do not give their money and practice stewardship, if a church is small because its people are indifferent to the lost, then how in the world can such a group be considered more spiritual than the church which is large because its people do believe and practice these things?

When I hear people say, "The church is too big already," I want to ask them, "Too big for what?" If there are people who want to attend our church because of its spirit, its fellowship, its opportunity for personal growth, its program, or its preaching, are the members to say, "We do not have any room for you and your family"?

When the crowds grew too large for Jesus to talk to a few at a time, did he send them away with instructions to go some other place? Of course not. He improvised. He got into a boat and pushed out from the shore so he could stand up and preach and a greater number of people could see him and hear him.

When the house in which he was preaching got overcrowded, did he tell the people outside that there was no more room for them, or did he stand there approvingly while they literally tore the roof off to get someone else in? Did Simon Peter tell the three thousand converts at Pentecost that some of them had to go somewhere else because the church was too large?

Let's get back to my rich friend. He did make a sizable contribution to our building. Just recently, he took me to lunch and confessed that he had been wrong about big churches. He had seen our church grow without losing its warmth and its personal touch. It took a big man to admit his mistake.

It is not the size of the church but the spirit of a church that counts. I know of some large churches that are alive and dynamic. I know of some little churches that are dull and dead. The size doesn't matter. The truth is that bigger churches usually can do a better job of evangelism and discipleship than smaller ones.

Dead but Not Buried

Most churches don't want to grow because of spiritual indifference. They have lost their vision and their sense of mission. They just don't care. They are so cold that you could ice-skate down their aisles.

George Bernard Shaw once said that the words on the tombstone of many people should read, "Died at thirty, buried at sixty." The same is true of many churches. They are dead and aren't even aware of it.

The indifferent church courts disaster. Jesus said to the lukewarm church at Laodicea, "I know that you are neither cold nor hot. How I wish you were either one or the other! But because you are lukewarm, neither hot nor cold, I am going to spit you out of my mouth!" (Rev. 3:15-16, TEV).

We cannot build a different world with an indifferent church. We must wake up and warm up if we are going to win people to the Savior.

Who's in Charge Here?

Growth can also be threatening. It not only means new buildings, new programs, and new staff members but also it means new people. In some instances, these new people pose a threat to the existing leadership of the church. Most older churches have a group of established leaders who have virtually run the church through the years. This is not always bad. Sometimes it has come about out of necessity. With the rapid turnover of pastors that occurs in most churches, there would be no continuity in the church program without these faithful lay people who take charge. The church would soon die.

But some of these leaders become too possessive. They are like the man who was showing a visitor around his community. He drove up in front of the church he attended, rolled the window down, and pointed to the sanctuary saying, "That's my church." The visitor responded, "Oh, do you belong to that church?" The man replied, "No, it belongs to me."

Such people are like Diotrephes, that member of the first-century church who, "loveth to have the preeminence among them" (3 John 9). Diotrephes was fond of being first. He delighted in running the church. He had such a stranglehold on the church that he was stifling its progress, and John had to deal with him severely. May our dear Lord deliver all of his churches from the descendants of Diotrephes, who satisfy their egos at the expense of God's work.

Stay a Little Longer

Pastors could do a lot more to help their churches grow if they would just stay in their pastorates longer. Preachers are notorious for staying on the move. Many churches have often seen a new pastor come to their church with fresh enthusiasm and innovative programs and just about the time things started he moved on. Having seen this again and again, churches are tired of that kind of roller-coaster program and prefer to do nothing.

Some churches have followed their leadership into larger programs only to have the leader move and leave them with nothing but big problems and big payments. Naturally, such churches are cautious.

Churches want to be sure about a continuity of leadership before they jump into something new. Our church recently elected a sanctuary expansion committee. When I met with the chairman to share my ideas, he said, "The first thing I want to know is, Do you plan to stay with us?" I can understand his concern. It was a fair question.

Continuity helps build the confidence which is necessary to get a church to launch out on something new. How long can a pastor stay at one church? Usually as long as he keeps dreaming, studying, working, and loving the people, and as long as the Lord wills.

There Is No Standing Still

As far as I am concerned, churches have no choice but to grow. The church that does not plan to grow, plans to fail. There is no standing still in any area of life. Churches which limit their growth begin a program of self-destruction. As someone has said, "We must either evangelize or fossilize." If a church is in a growing area and the church does not grow, it is sick. There is something critically wrong with it.

The New Testament is in favor of growth. The history of the early church is punctuated by such phrases as, "The Lord added to the church daily" (Acts 2:47); "The number of the disciples was multiplied" (Acts 6:1); "A great company of the priests were obedient to the faith" (Acts 6:7); "A great number believed" (Acts 11:21).

Added! Multiplied! Great numbers! These words characterized the life of the early church and ought to characterize the life of our churches also.

Choosing Your Method

Once a church has made a commitment to growth, it must then decide how it is going to grow. What methods will it use? Some churches choose to grow by gimmicks. I was in a church recently that was promoting an attendance contest among its bus riders. The driver of the bus that had the fewest riders on a given Sunday was going to have to kiss a pig. Such sideshow antics cheapen the gospel and produce no spiritual depth. From what I saw and heard, the pig didn't even like it. He squealed all the while.

Other churches choose to grow on the strength of the charismatic personality of their leader. But such growth is not lasting either. When the leader leaves, the crowds leave with him.

What methods, then, shall we use? For years, I've been a student of church growth. I have learned that the great and growing churches do not do anything unusual. They do the usual unusually well. They preach well; they teach well; they pray well; and they visit well.

If you want to build your church on a foundation of cement rather than shaving cream, I suggest that you build it on the basics also. We must not be committed to growth at any cost. Unless growth can come in such a way as to honor God and is consistent with the New Testament, we do not need to grow. If preaching, teaching, visiting, praying, and good programs won't reach people, then let the church die. But don't worry, the church won't die if it sticks with these things.

If you desire to grow in this way, I suggest that you find a church that is growing by these same basics and visit it.

Set up a conference with its pastor. Ask to be placed on their mailing list. Look over their facilities. Attend their worship services. As baseball coach Yogi Berra said, "You can observe a lot by just watching." Successful people do not follow the example of failures.

When you have listened to and learned from others, develop your own program and get going. But hurry before sundown. "The night cometh when no man can work" (John 9:4).

3
The Crisis of Leadership

The most important factor in determining whether a church grows or declines is its leadership. Churches almost never rise above their leaders. That means then that the greatest crisis of the church today is a need for bold, dynamic, aggressive leadership.

Fred Smith, a business management consultant, said to a group of us some time ago, "I visit thirty or forty churches a year, and most of them are dead. The reason they are dead is that the preacher is dead." John R. Mott, the great missionary-statesman said, "Whenever the church has failed, it has failed because of inadequate leadership."

Many people do not really understand what leadership is. It is the ability to rally people to a common cause. There are two things about leadership that we must keep constantly before us. First, it is local. Second, it is full time. By *local* I mean that we cannot look to the head office of our denomination for leadership. They do not know our fields, our specific needs, or our people. By full time, I mean that we cannot look to the deacons or any other volunteer group in the church to give leadership. They are not on the scene enough to know all that needs to be done.

If the church is going to have leadership, preachers are going to have to give it. Ernest P. Campbell, former pastor of the Riverside Church in New York City, has suggested a new beatitude, "Blessed are those who fill the positions they occupy."

Those of us who are in places of leadership must begin to give bold and dynamic leadership to our churches if we are going to grow. We need to do what Paul told Timothy to do, "Stir up the gift of God which is in thee" (2 Tim. 1:6). The gift Paul referred to was the gift of pastoral leadership. Timothy had the gift of leadership but he was not using it. Obviously, Timothy was insecure and timid. He may even have suffered from an inferiority complex. Instead of being the bold, daring leader he was supposed to be, he was shy and reserved.

So, Paul told Timothy to "stir up" his gift. The word *stir* means "to fan again to flames." It is a picture of a fire that once blazed brightly but is now cooling out. There is nothing left but a bed of hot coals. If fanned, they would burst into flames again. Timothy had grown cold and indifferent in God's service. The fire had gone out of his life. He needed to rekindle the flames of leadership.

That's what we need today. We need to be stirred to new dedication, new zeal, and new enthusiasm in leading God's people.

Paul went on to say to Timothy, "For God hath not given us the spirit of fear; but of power, and of love, and of a sound mind" (2 Tim. 1:7). God doesn't want us to be timid or cowardly. So he has given us all the abilities we need to be dynamic leaders. He has given us "power," the strength by which we are to lead. He has given us "love," the spirit in which we are to lead. And he has given us a "sound mind," the good sense with which we are to lead. Strength! Spirit! Sense! What else do we need? Now, we must use those abilities to their fullest if we want our churches to grow.

What are the marks of a good leader? What qualities does it take to lead a church to grow? There are six of them that I want you to consider.

The Vision to See

The first characteristic of a good leader is vision. Vision is not so much the ability to see the unseen as it is the ability to see the obvious, which ordinary people overlook. Vision is seeing what needs to be done and how best to do it.

Vision usually takes the form of a dream, a burden, or a great challenge. Vision gives our lives and our churches purpose, mission, and destiny.

What a powerful force dreams are. Look around you! Everything that now is was at one time a dream in somebody's mind. Because they held that dream before them, they eventually found a way to make their dreams come true. And if you hold your dreams before you, they will soon translate themselves into energy and you will find yourself doing what you have been dreaming about.

You might think that the world is full of dreamers, people of vision, people who think. But not so! Brain power is always in far less supply than manpower. There are not many who think, who see, and who dream.

It is the role of leadership to get a vision from God, to dream dreams, to develop plans, and then to communicate those things convincingly to people. The problem is that most churches aren't getting that. Most leaders seem to have no purpose or goal beyond meeting next Sunday. That's why our churches are lagging behind. They are dying from sameness. Business as usual will not get the job done.

Great movements are built in response to a challenge. So we must give our churches a challenge and bold leadership. It is still true that "where there is no vision, the people perish" (Prov. 29:18).

It is not enough just to think, dream, and plan. We must think big, dream big, and plan big. Little plans have no power to stir souls. If plans are so small that they present no challenge, people will yawn, turn the plans off like an alarm clock, turn over, and go back to sleep.

The great evangelist D. L. Moody scribbled in the margin of his Bible adjacent to the experience of Jesus feeding the five thousand, "If God be your partner make no little plans." I'm persuaded that if plans are not big enough to stagger the imagination, they will not be big enough to trigger the enthusiasm of the people.

People can't respond to nothing. We must give them something to respond to. The preacher's job is to catch a vision of winning our world to Christ, building a new building, adding additional staff, saturating the community with the gospel, going on television, or undertaking some other great work for God and challenging the people to move forward.

Don't underestimate your people. Most preachers would be surprised at the response of their people if they would just lay before them a great vision and challenge.

When I shared our plans to evangelize Belize with a fellow pastor, he said, "This looks to me like a twenty-year project." That's a large part of our problem. We are thinking twenty years when we ought to be thinking five years. We are taking the easy way out. We aren't challenging people enough.

When I shared the challenge of evangelizing Belize with my people, not one of them expressed doubt. They made a wholehearted response. It makes me believe the problem is with those of us who are leaders and not with our people.

Within six months, our people had given or pledged a hundred thousand dollars and six different individuals had pledged to build churches by themselves. A visitor in our worship services that day sent a check for twenty-five hundred dollars to buy Bibles. A Methodist from another city who had been attending our single adult Sunday School class sent two checks totaling six thousand dollars. A medical doctor gave nine thousand dollars in memory of his son who had recently died. One of our young deacons sold a piece of land for six thousand dollars. He and his wife had intended to use the profits as a nest egg for the future. Instead they decided to give the money to Belize. Another man pledged five thousand dollars a year for the next five years. Stories like this can be multiplied again and again. It is an evidence of what people can and will do if they are challenged.

We must challenge our people to do great things; otherwise, we will stagnate into mediocrity.

I think mediocrity is one of the cardinal sins of Christianity. It has quenched the power of the Holy Spirit and has often been enshrined as our patron saint. I am extremely incensed at the "bold" planning of cautious Christians. Mediocrity is the seeing-eye dog of blind Christians who are trying to walk by sight. "If everybody is doing it, it must be good," should be, "If everybody is doing it, it is not good enough for the Master's minority."

The Faith to Try

Faith is also necessary to being a good leader. It is not enough to have vision to see; we must also have faith to try. Faith is the confident assurance in God that sets us free to attempt the impossible. It is believing so much in God that we are set free from the shackles of fear, doubt, and pessimism that so often immobilize us.

The Scriptures define faith as "the substance of things hoped for, the evidence of things not seen" (Heb. 11:1). Since faith has to do with things "hoped for" and things "not seen," it must always involve an element of risk. Things hoped for have not yet been realized. Things unseen have not yet been visualized. So, there must ever and always be that element of chance in faith.

The best illustration of faith I know of is out of the life of the apostle Paul. He was on a ship sailing for Rome when his ship was caught in a storm. For several days, the little ship was tossed by the wind and the waves. After days of not seeing the sun by day nor the moon by night, the captain and the crew became convinced that all hope was gone. They believed that the ship was going to sink. Just as panic was about to break out on the ship, the apostle Paul spoke up and told them not to be afraid. An angel of the Lord had appeared to Paul and assured him that no person on the ship would lose his life. Then Paul said, "Wherefore, sirs, be of good cheer: for I believe God, that it shall be even as it was told me" (Acts 27:25).

That's faith! Faith is believing in God in spite of the circumstances. Faith is believing God even in the middle of the storm. Faith is believing God regardless of the unanimous opinion of experts. Faith is believing in God in spite of weather reports.

Do not confuse faith with positive thinking. They are not the same thing. I believe in positive thinking. I like to be around optimistic, positive people. They encourage me. This is especially true since most of the barriers in life are mental. As someone has said, "Anything conceivable and believable is achievable."

Let me illustrate. Before 1954, no one had ever run a mile in less than four minutes. Then in 1954, Roger Bannister did it. Once he did it, other runners saw that it was possible; now it has been done hundreds of times. The barrier was mental.

It is that way in all of life. Most of the barriers of life are mental or psychological, and positive thinking enables us to conquer most of them. But faith is different. Positive thinking is human-centered while faith is God-centered. Positive thinking is believing in what *I* can do. Faith is believing in what *God* can do.

If our churches are going to grow, we must have leaders of faith, people who are willing to launch out and take risks. We are going to have to attempt things that are beyond our ability.

Shortly after we built our Family Life Center, I met a banker from another church while I was shopping. He asked me how we were doing. I told him that we were ready to move into our Family Life Center and that our people had already given $325,000 in pledges. His church had been thinking about building such a building for some time, so he said, "If we had $325,000, we would build a building." I replied, "Build the building, and you will get your $325,000."

People don't give half as much money to a building you are talking about as they do to one you are building. We must take the step of faith before we can see results. Without faith it is impossible to please the Lord.

The Enthusiasm to Care

Mark Twain, when asked the secret of his success, said, "I was more excited." All good leaders and all successful people are enthusiastic. There is no more powerful force on earth than a human soul on fire.

What is enthusiasm? It is not a rah-rah-rah attitude that goes around saying "Praise the Lord" all the time. It is a combination of excitement, energy, and expectancy.

Where does enthusiasm come from? It comes from

two sources. It comes from the spirit of God within us. In fact, the word *enthusiasm* literally means "God in us." So enthusiasm is not just something we whip up. It is something we draw out. It is already there, and we just turn it loose. If the living God is within you, you ought to be excited. Your soul ought to be on fire.

Enthusiasm also comes from our vision or our dreams. Buzz Aldrin, the second man who walked on the moon, came back to the earth and had a nervous breakdown. He explained his breakdown in part by saying, "When you have achieved all of your goals, depression sets in." You can't get excited about nothing. Show me a church or a pastor who is dull and depressed and I will show you a church or a pastor who has stopped dreaming, setting goals, and having visions.

Enthusiasm is essential to leadership. It boils down to this: We need to either get excited or get out. To paraphrase Charles Jarvis, one of the world's foremost humorists, "A leader who is not fired with enthusiasm ought to be fired . . . with enthusiasm!"

The Energy to Work

The best way to make your dreams come true is to wake up and go to work. Great Christian leaders have always been people with enormous energy. They are people who have lived like saints and have worked like the devil.

The apostle Paul had many gifts. He had a keen mind, a thick hide, a warm heart, and a strong faith. But he never once suggested that those gifts were a substitute for hard work. In fact, Paul explained the success of his ministry in part by saying that he just plainly worked harder than all the other apostles (1 Cor. 15:10).

There is no substitute for hard work. But, on the other

hand, hard work will make up for almost any other deficiency one may have. One doesn't have to have the keenest mind, the most charming personality, or the most eloquent voice to do great things for God. If you will work harder than other people, you will probably accomplish more for God.

Sidney J. Harris, the philosopher, said, "There is geometric progression in ability: you need to be only ten percent better to go one-hundred percent further."

Many of us have long admired R. G. Lee, the late pastor of the Bellevue Baptist Church, Memphis, Tennessee, for the great work he did. In his ministry, Lee wrote fifty-three books and averaged twelve visits to church members and prospects per day—that's right, per day. He baptized converts every Sunday. There is no way to explain his great success unless you include in it the element of hard work.

The problem with many people today is that they confuse motion with action. They don't know the difference between kicking up dust and shoveling dirt.

Laziness is going to kill us. Many preachers get up late, piddle around the house, take the kids to school, meander down to the office, read their mail, drink coffee with some friends, and then go back to the office until lunchtime. In the afternoon, they pick up the kids from school, "baby-sit" while their wives go to the beauty parlor, and then drop by the hospital to make a few visits. By then the day is over, and they have done almost nothing but waste time.

We need to get up on time. We need to get into our studies and labor at the Word and doctrine (1 Tim. 5:17-18). We need to make a set number of visits each day. We need to work, work, work. And if we do, the people will know it, respect us for it, and more likely follow our leadership.

We need to take a day off to rest every week. Everybody needs that, but we need to work more than we do. Long ago an ancient Greek wrote, "The gates of excellence are always surrounded by a sea of sweat." And as my evangelistic singer friend Fritz Smith told me, "The only place where success comes before work is in the dictionary."

It's high time the servants of God stop sitting around twiddling their thumbs. We need to roll up our sleeves and go to work. I'm not talking about attending so many committee meetings that you get an ingrown shirttail. I'm referring to witnessing and ministering and serving in the name of the Lord Jesus Christ wherever you are.

Skill to Motivate

Leadership must be personable, perceptive, persuasive, and practical. Leaders must love people and be able to motivate them.

Leadership in the church differs from leadership in the military, in business, or in athletics. In those areas, leadership is by force, by voted authority, and by position. In the church, leadership must lead by example, influence, and love. Preachers are working with volunteer help and are operating on free-will offerings. Pastoral leadership cannot be demanded. It is earned.

It is earned by the sheer force of a wise, loving, discerning personality. It will be determined by the quality of your faith, the strength of your personality, the depth of your commitment to Christ, the sweetness of your spirit, and the clarity of your presentation.

As a leader you are the catalyst of the church. You must be a self-starter and be a good motivator. Eddie Arcaro, the famous jockey, said, "Horses are like people. Most of them will dog it and goof off if you let them get away with it. At least seventy percent of all race horses don't want to win."

People must be motivated also. Of course, we can't drive them like horses, but we can inspire them.

Making announcements is not leadership. People must be organized so that they understand clearly what their responsibilities are. Nothing becomes dynamic until it becomes specific. Let me illustrate. I've been in many revival meetings where the pastor became inspired halfway through the revival and suddenly announced a challenging goal for Sunday School the following Sunday. But he did nothing beyond that announcement. He thought he was giving bold leadership, but he was really giving no leadership at all. First, the people who needed to hear his announcement weren't there. So, they didn't even know about the goal.

Secondly, those who were there had no idea what their part in reaching the goal was. Leaders must be able to set clear goals, break those goals down into specific assignments, and then motivate people to do their part.

Determine to Stick

You can't have a backbone of gelatin and be a good leader. You must have the courage and determination to withstand criticism, pessimism, and indifference.

Don't expect smooth sailing. Opposition will come to any effective Christian leader, not only from the enemies of Christ but also sometimes from the leader's friends. Ministers will tolerate almost anything from one another except success or failure. If you fall on your face, they will condemn you. If you succeed, they will become jealous and critical of you. It is only if you are brilliantly mediocre that they will accept you.

To be a good leader, you must refuse to be diverted

from your appointed task. There will always be the hecklers who hurl snide remarks at you as they did at Nehemiah (Neh. 6:3). Nehemiah undertook the great task of rebuilding the walls of the city of Jerusalem. You would think that all the people would rally around him and support him in this great effort. But not so. On every hand, he met with resistance and disappointment.

Nehemiah was constantly beset by hecklers who wanted to get him into a conversation. He steadfastly refused, saying, "I am doing a great work, so that I cannot come down: why should the work cease, while I leave it and come down to you?"

Persistency has characterized all great leaders. Prime Minister Begin of Israel ran for the office of prime minister nine times before he was elected. He persisted with dogged determination; he refused to give up and quit. The result is that, at this writing, he has become one of the most influential men in the world today.

Vision, faith, enthusiasm, energy, skill, and determination are the qualities we absolutely need if we are to become effective leaders.

Wilt Thou Be Made Whole?

If you aren't a leader now, you can be. The question Jesus asked the crippled man was, "Wilt thou be made whole?" (John 5:6). That at first seems to be a foolish question. However, the more you think about it the more you realize how basic it really is. If you don't want to be different badly enough to change, you never will be. You can become an effective leader for Christ even if you aren't one now, if you want to be. The real question is "Wilt thou. . . ."

4
What Makes a Church Grow?

I'm often asked, "What is the secret to your church's continuous growth?" There is, of course, no one answer to that question.

Some people try to explain our growth by saying, "You just happen to be in the right place at the right time." There is no doubt that this helps, but there is more to it than that. I can show you other churches around us that serve the same neighborhood, believe the same Bible, and have the same opportunity that we do, but they are not growing. To the contrary, they are declining.

John Wooden, the legendary basketball coach from UCLA, whose teams won ten national championships in eleven years, once said, "Nobody can win without talent. But not everyone can win with talent."

There are factors beyond location that affect church growth just as there are things other than talent that make for a winning basketball team. To ignore these factors is to commit ecclesiastical suicide.

Some of the things that we have done have just come naturally as an expression of our personalities. Others we have learned by reading about successful churches, talking to successful leaders, and by trial and error.

Here are the seven things that have contributed most to our church's growth.

Build a Sweet Spirit

Without a doubt, the single most important explanation, humanly speaking, of the growth of our church is the spirit of our people. There is in our church a spirit of love, joy, friendliness, and excitement.

Our people love the Lord and his church. They are proud of it, loyal to it, and excited about it. They honestly believe that ours is the greatest church in the world. They also believe that we can and will do anything that we set out to do. And, you know what? I think they are right.

Though our church is large and growing larger, we have maintained a small-church atmosphere. We go out of our way to make people feel welcome. We want people to feel loved and accepted the first time they come to visit us. We live in a cold world, and people are drawn by the warmth of Christian love.

This friendly spirit begins with our staff and filters down throughout the whole congregation. Our staff mixes with our people, and they feel comfortable around us. There are no prima donnas among us. We talk together, laugh together, and genuinely enjoy being together.

We do not try to impress people with how smart we are, how holy we are, or how dignified we are. To us the church is the family of God (1 Tim. 3:15), and the gathering of the church is like a family reunion. A spirit of informality and friendliness permeates all we do.

This makes worship a happy experience. Our services are like celebrations. That's the way it ought to be. Jesus was a happy, fun-loving person. In fact, he compared himself to a bridegroom and his followers to wedding guests. That means that worship ought to be more like a wedding than like a wake. Staff members ought to act more like groomsmen than pallbearers. The world has enough sadness already without the church adding to it. Going to church ought to be fun.

Our music sets the tone of the services. It is alive, exciting, and triumphant. You can't build a church on music, but you can't build a church without music. Our announcements sound more like a sportscast than a funeral eulogy, and the preaching is biblical, relevant, authoritative, and dynamic.

My associate pastor, John LaNoue, says, "I find that relevance is a missing link between preaching from the pulpit and the performance of the people in the pews. The applicator is missing out of most ministerial medicine bottles."

There is a spontaneity in all that we do. Humor is injected if it seems appropriate. I do not hesitate to change our order of service on the spur of the moment if there is some hymn I feel we should sing. I tease our staff members openly, and they tease back. This freedom, this spontaneity, is very important in building a happy, relaxed spirit. These things do not detract from worship. They enhance it. They help the people relax and be receptive to God's word.

As a visitor said to me last Sunday, "It's evident that your church is just one great, big, happy family." He was right; that's why we are growing.

We communicate our love to people in every way possible. When people start down the aisle to make a decision for Christ, I don't wait at the front with folded arms for them to come to me. I go up the aisle and meet them halfway. I shake hands with them and, with my arm around their shoulders, we walk the rest of the way down the aisle together. We usually close our services by asking the people to join hands across the aisles and to sing a triumphant hymn, such as "Victory In Jesus" or "When We All Get to Heaven."

Some people, like widows and divorcees, never touch another person in a meaningful way throughout the whole week. This kind of touching communicates love and warmth. We genuinely love one another and like to be with one another. That's why our church is growing.

Our people carry this feeling of love and joy and excitement with them wherever they go. They are quick to tell others about the church they love. As a result, they are constantly inviting friends, neighbors, and even strangers to our church. Studies indicate that 80 percent of the people who join a church do so because they were introduced by friends. The record of our church shows this to be true.

Because of all of this, Green Acres enjoys a good reputation in our city. People know we are here. They believe our church is where the action is. They think we can get things done.

Recently, the directors of an exclusive club in our community decided to relocate and enlarge their facilities. When they learned that the project would cost approximately one million dollars, some of the members expressed pessimism about raising that much money. Finally one of them spoke up and said, "Why, Green Acres Baptist Church wouldn't bat an eye at a million-dollar project. They could raise that much money in one day."

When I heard that, I said, "Hallelujah! For once the church is the steam engine and not the caboose of progress." That's the way it ought to be. The church ought to be the most progressive, alive, dynamic place in town.

I can't stress too much the importance of a church's reputation. If it is known about the community as a growing, happy, loving place, people will want to come.

What kind of reputation does your church have in the community? What do people outside the church think of you? It is a key factor in your growth.

Be Bible Centered

Our entire program is built around the Bible. We believe that it is God's inspired Word, and its authority is unquestioned. It is preached in the pulpit, taught in the classroom, believed in the pew, and lived in the streets.

As a result, people by the scores are coming to our church from other denominations that might have forsaken the Scriptures for other issues and I am not a proselyter. Those people are coming of their own volition.

In fact, we have so many people coming to our church from other denominations that I wrote and printed a brief doctrinal statement for our church called "Where We Stand." It is longer than a tract and smaller than a book. I give it to people who are considering joining our church. It has proven to be an invaluable tool in reaching people of other denominations. I think every church ought to have its own doctrinal statement. A copy of this statement is included in the appendixes.

A few years ago a family that belonged to another denomination visited our morning worship services. That afternoon, as is my custom, I called them to welcome them to our services. As we talked, the lady said, "I love the way you preach the Bible. Do you do that often?" I told her that I do it every Sunday morning and every Sunday night, and every Wednesday night. Then she said, "Oh, I need that."

Doesn't everybody need to hear the Bible preached? But they aren't getting it. Her family wasn't and that's why a few weeks later they all joined us by baptism.

I read recently of a large church that was offering a

course on interior decorating during its Sunday evening training hour. Can you imagine the apostle Paul teaching a course on interior decorating to the Philippian jailer? Not on your life! Paul taught him about Christ. When the jailer was converted he may have initiated his own program of prison reform.

Growing churches are Bible-centered churches. If you want your church to grow, magnify the Word of God.

Put the Pulpit in the Center

If you were to walk into our sanctuary, one glance would reveal why our church is growing. The pulpit is at the front and center of the platform. This arrangement of the furniture tells you that preaching is central in our church. So important is preaching to the growth of our church that a whole chapter in this book is devoted to it. It is sufficient to say here that growing churches are always characterized by a strong pulpit ministry.

Give Them Service and Selection

A good program is another key to our growth. We strive to have the best music ministry, recreation ministry, Youth ministry, Single Adult ministry, retreat ministry, senior citizen ministry, and childhood ministry possible.

Sunday School and worship services alone will no longer get the job done. Some people are looking for a Youth ministry and will be attracted to your church if you take care of their young people. And, with the graying of America there are more and more senior citizens. These elderly people are not only a tremendous asset to the church but also have special needs. Many of them are still in good health and have an abundance of time and energy. Provide a program for them, and they can be reached.

In our recreation ministry, we have twelve softball

teams, twenty intramural volleyball teams, and twenty-nine intramural basketball teams. In addition, we have craft classes, bowling leagues, racquetball tournaments, weight-lifting classes, and exercise classes. These activities attract many people, young and old, to our church.

For awhile, about the only place in our community where singles could go to meet other singles was a bar. So we decided to provide an alternative. We set aside an area in our church as a "singles center." We decorated it with living room furniture, a television, game table, soft drink machine, popcorn popper, and coffee urn. We enlisted a staff of volunteers who keep it open six nights a week from 6:00 PM to 10:00 PM, and on weekends from 1:00 PM to 10:00 PM.

Our singles know that if they want to get out of their apartments they can always come to the singles center in our church and people will be there to visit with them. If nothing else, they can just watch television with another warm body in the same room. The result is that our Single Adult ministry is growing by leaps and bounds.

"But," you say, "we can't afford to do things like that." I'm not sure you can afford not to. Growth costs, but so does death. Have you priced a good funeral lately?

We cannot operate in the twentieth century with horse-and-buggy programs. The church that grows is the church which presents a well-rounded program, meeting the needs of all the people. When I was a boy, I often visited my grandparents' little one-room church in the country. For Sunday School, the men met in one corner, the women in another, the children in another, and the young people in another. We sat on wooden slat benches, sang by the light of Coleman lanterns, and fanned ourselves with funeral home fans. When the preacher finished his sermon, if he could talk above a whisper and wasn't walking on three inches of his pants' legs, the people felt that he hadn't preached a lick.

That sort of program was good enough for them, but you can't attract people to that kind of situation today. The world is changing, and we must change with it. The church has to keep up or it will lose out.

Do you remember the neighborhood grocery stores that used to be so common in America? One was located within walking distance of almost every home. They had a limited selection of merchandise, the owner knew you by name, and he would even charge your groceries on your own personal charge book.

But where is the neighborhood grocery store now? It has been replaced by the supermarket. The supermarket is not within walking distance of your home, and the manager will seldom know your name. He will hardly cash your check, much less charge anything to you. Still, you go there because it offers you a larger selection and better service.

Service and selection is what people are looking for. People don't change that much just because it is Sunday morning. They will still put service and selection above convenience. The church that provides these things is the church that is going to grow.

Go After People

Visitation and outreach are primary in our church. A good portion of our congregation is involved in these activities.

Visitation is carried on by our staff, by individuals, through small groups, by special teams, and especially through our Sunday School.

Several years ago a neighboring pastor was trying to justify the lack of growth in his own church and explained away the growth of our church when he said, "You get a lot of walk-ins at Green Acres."

He could not be further from the truth. People don't just walk into our church. If they did, they would have to pass several other churches in order to get there. They come because we first go out to visit them.

Our church is growing because we give priority to outreach.

Ministry and Missions

Our church invests heavily in both local and foreign missions. Through giving, mission trips, a missionary home, a foster home, a retreat center, a senior citizens' ministry, rest home, and chest hospital services, our church is carrying out the Great Commission.

Through church building, mission trips—in particular our missions commitment to Belize—we are seeking to witness to the ends of the earth.

There is a close correlation between a church's growth at home and its vision and commitment to a needy world. The more we get outside ourselves to minister to others the more we grow.

Our primary concern should never be our own growth. It should be missions and ministry for Christ. Growth comes as a by-product of these. The more we do these things the more we grow ourselves. It works this way—when we take care of God's Word, he takes care of our growth. The growth of a plant depends on three things: the seed, the soil, and the seasons. Missions and ministry create the kind of warm climate in a church that makes growth possible.

Keep the Power Lines Up

Much emphasis is placed on prayer in our church. The Holy Spirit is the life of our church. We are not dynamos but conductors of power. He is the source.

Through preaching, studies, prayer breakfasts, prayer chains, prayer groups, days of prayer, and especially prayer meetings, we emphasize prayer. We work as though everything depends on us, and we pray as if everything depends on God. That's why we are growing.

Recently, we had an ice storm in our community. As a result power lines were down and transformers were out. For several days large sections of our city were without electricity. Some of our people had to heat their homes with fireplaces and light them with kerosene lamps. As one of our families sat in the living room reading by a kerosene lamp, the wife looked up at a beautiful and expensive chandelier and said to her husband, "That's about the most useless thing I've ever seen."

Many of our people came to realize that chandeliers, clocks, toasters, can openers, TV's, and dishwashers were of little value without power.

It is the same with our churches. All else that we do is useless unless the power of the Lord is there.

You must keep the power lines of prayer up and working if you want your church to grow.

These, I believe, are the key factors to growth in our church or in any church.

But I hear some people saying, "Well, all of that is fine and good at Green Acres, but . . . if we had your people, your location, your resources, your staff, we'd so something . . . but. . . ."

If you aren't careful, the first thing you know you will have "butted" yourself out of business. We need execution and not excuses. These are the key factors to growth in our church. I believe they will work in your church also.

5
The Primacy of Preaching

After I left my last pastorate, Vernon McDonald, a college basketball coach whom I had won to Christ, was elected to serve on the pulpit (or pastor-search) committee. He had been a Christian for only five years, and this was an eye-opening experience for him. The committee visited between fifteen and twenty churches before they found a preacher they wanted. Vernon listened intently to a multitude of preachers for the first time since his conversion.

When his job was over, he said to me, "Paul, our churches are in trouble. Preachers aren't doing much good preaching. Most of the time they just stand up, flip the pages of their notebooks, and read their sermons without any enthusiasm."

Since that time I have talked with many other pulpit committee members who have said essentially the same thing. If their observation is right, it largely explains why so few churches are growing.

Preaching has always been the minister's greatest opportunity and responsibility. Preaching is a barometer of the life of the church. When preaching is dynamic, the church is strong; when it is insipid, the church is weak.

I am not overstating the case when I say that it is with preaching that churches grow or decline. If you want your church to grow, give attention to preaching. Make sure you are preaching well-prepared, Bible-based sermons that are well illustrated and delivered in a dynamic way.

Be a Man's Man

Effective preaching begins with what you are. You can never separate the person from his message. What you preach flows from what you are. So you need, first of all, to be your best if you want to influence others. Next to a genuine commitment to Christ and a holy life, this will determine your effectiveness.

Join the human race. Act normal. Smile a little. Sprinkle some humor into your sermons. You can't take the ministry too seriously, but you surely can take yourself too seriously.

Preaching That Helps

There are several things that characterize the kind of preaching that helps churches to grow.

Know Your Material

First, your sermons ought to be well prepared. Paul told Timothy, "Study to shew thyself approved unto God, a workman that needeth not to be ashamed, rightly dividing the word of truth" (2 Tim. 2:15). The Greek word translated *divide* means to cut a straight line. It describes a farmer who sets his eyes on a distant object and plows a straight furrow to it.

Good preaching can't wander all over the place or chase every rabbit that it passes. It must have a clear objective and move quickly toward it. In this informed and educated age, the preacher can ill afford to go into the pulpit unprepared. He can't expect people to come and hear him when he doesn't know what he is talking about or where he is going.

A sermon is a solemn responsibility. With all of my other duties, I can make no more than a dozen or so personal calls every week. But in our two worship services on Sunday morning I have the undivided attention of two thousand people for at least thirty minutes. For this reason, I must do my homework.

If I preach a bad sermon, I'm wasting not only a half hour of my own time, but also I have wasted one thousand hours of the congregation's time. That is more than forty days and forty nights!

I must, therefore, give careful attention to sermon preparation during the week so I can preach effectively on Sunday. In preparing a sermon, the first thing I do is decide on the theme. What does God want me to say? What do my people need to hear? Then I select a text. Often these two come simultaneously. At times the text comes first and suggests the theme. Then I carefully make an exegesis of the passage. What do the words mean? What is the background to the passage? What is God actually saying? Then I try to divide the text into two, three, or four logical divisions and find several good illustrations to throw light on the subject.

Sermon preparation is seldom easy for me. It requires hours and hours of work. I take comfort, however, in the fact that if the message is of little cost to the preacher, it will be of little value to the congregation.

The reward of prayer, study, and soul saturation is heavenly. The ordinary preacher becomes a great preacher. R. G. Lee said, "You cannot live on skimmed milk during the days of the week and preach cream on Sunday."

Someone has summarized the qualifications for a good speaker this way: "Know your stuff! Know whom you're stuffing! Then stuff them!" That's good advice for the preacher.

Illustrate Well

Your sermon should also be well illustrated. Illustrations are like windows. They let light into the chambers of the mind. But more than that, they add a breath of fresh air that will help keep people awake.

If people are going to sleep during your sermons, you are the one who needs to wake up.

Carl Sandburg was persuaded to attend a dress rehearsal of a very serious play by a serious young dramatist. Unfortunately, he slept through the greater part of the performance. The outraged dramatist chided him later by saying, "How could you sleep through my play when you knew how much I wanted your opinion?"

"Young man," Sandburg said, "sleep is an opinion."

A sleeping congregation will never be a growing one. I often tell people I visit, "It's your job to come to church and it's my job to keep you awake. If you'll do your part, I'll promise to do mine." I really mean that, and I do my very best to keep my promise.

There is no excuse for a dull sermon. Andrew W. Blackwood was right when he said, "A good sermon should be as exciting as a baseball game."

When I have to sit through a dull, boring sermon, I feel like Harry Emerson Fosdick who said, "The surprising thing is not that so few people come to church. The surprising thing is that anyone comes at all."

Yesterday a young pastor from a neighboring community came to visit me. He asked, "Where do you get your illustrations and how do you file them away for future use?" I find illustrations everywhere—in magazines, in newspapers, from listening to other preachers, and from everyday experiences. I file these in manila folders under the appropriate subject.

When I started preaching, I could not afford an elaborate filing system. So I bought twenty-six manila folders, printed one letter of the alphabet on each folder, put them in a cardboard box and started filing illustrations by their subject. In time, as my file grew thicker and thicker, I divided my material. Instead of one general folder under *s*, I now have a number of folders under *s*, dealing with such subjects as salvation, sin, security, success, second coming, Satan, and sex.

Illustrations are everywhere. It just takes time to develop an eye for them and to build a backlog of them. The preacher who doesn't use good illustrations is destined to be a dry and boring preacher.

Speak with Authority

Effective preaching must be delivered with a note of authority. Several years ago I preached a funeral service of a man who had not attended church regularly. As I stood at the head of the casket and the family viewed the body, the man's little eight-year-old son walked up to me, tugged on my sleeve and said, "Mister, are you God?"

The question caught me by surprise. After a moment I replied, "No, son, I'm not God. But I work for him, and I know him quite well."

When you preach, if people don't get the idea that you work for God and know him quite well, your preaching will not have the authority it ought to have.

Where does the preacher's authority come from? It comes from the fact that he is called by God, walks with God, and listens to God who gives him the right to speak for Him.

Paul admonished Timothy, "Preach the word" (2 Tim. 4:2). The word *preach* literally means "to herald." A herald was an official representative of the king whose responsibility it was to deliver the king's message to the people. His message had the same authority as if the king himself were there speaking to them.

We are the heralds of God. We are to preach his word with that kind of authority.

Proclaim God's Message

Fourth, you should preach the Bible. You should tell people what God says.

While making a prospect visit one night, a man asked our associate pastor, "What kind of Bible does your pastor use?" Of course he had reference to the translation that I use. My associate replied, "He uses the Holy Bible."

I don't care which translation you use. Just be sure you preach God's holy word. It alone is the eternal truth we need.

Every day, people are bombarded with what a politician says, what a psychiatrist says, what a psychologist says, what an editor says, what a commentator says, and what a man on the street says. But, what we would like to know is: Does God say anything? This is the assignment of the preacher. And, when he delivers that message faithfully and well, the people are marvelously blessed.

Do you remember the cry of King Zedekiah to the prophet Jeremiah: "Is there any word from the Lord?" Jeremiah replied, "There is" (Jer. 37:17). Preacher, for God's sake, tell us what God says. That is what we long to hear. What we need to hear. What we want to hear.

Some preachers ask, "Must I limit myself to the Bible?" That's like a minnow asking, "Must I limit myself to the Pacific Ocean?" Yes, limit yourself to the Bible. You should draw illustrations and facts from any and all sources, but your message should always be Bible based.

Let Your Humanity Show

A good sermon should unashamedly be strongly auto-biographical. Like the Bible itself, it should be a testimony.

More and more my preaching contains an element of confession in it. I share with people my own struggles, frustrations, and needs, as well as the victories of my life. Too long preachers have been afraid to confess that they are tempted, that they fail, that they sometimes get discouraged and want to quit. We have felt that we have to present a perfect image to our people.

Even the Bible doesn't do that. Barnabas confessed that he and Paul were "men of like passions" as the rest of us (Acts 14:15). James declared the same thing about Elijah (Jas. 5:17).

The word *passions* means "emotions, feelings, affections." Barnabas was confessing his humanness. He was saying that he and Paul were human beings with the same feelings, affections, and emotions as everyone else.

We preachers sometimes leave the impression that we are so dedicated that when we have a headache we take nothing but *St. Joseph's* aspirin. Thus, we increase the hurt of people by acting as if we never hurt.

Longfellow said, "Some must lead, some must follow, but all have feet of clay." I have discovered that people identify with my weaknesses more than with my strengths. Everyone has weaknesses. But not everyone is so sure that he has strengths.

The Sunday before Christmas, I preached a sermon on depression. In it I shared with our people the fact that I am occasionally depressed. That afternoon, a radio listener who identified with those same feelings wrote me a beautiful letter. She said in part:

Your message this morning has greatly touched my heart. I needed to be reminded why I am depressed today, why I am feeling so "down" at the most joyous season of the year, and most of all how I can cope with my feelings. . . . I just wanted you to know that your message "hit home" with me.

God loves you and is using you in a very special way to minister to GABC people. I'm thankful that you can also share your weaknesses and personal experiences with us too. Paul Powell is human and God loves you in spite of all of your weaknesses. Only God is perfect.

Don't be afraid to confess your struggles and hardships. It will strengthen others who are going through the same kind of experiences.

Preach for a Verdict

Finally, a good sermon is one that gives you something to feel, something to remember, and something to do. It has been said that an essay is directed to the mind; a poem is directed to the imagination; a drama is directed to the emotions. But preaching is directed to all three with the intent of getting at the will and gaining a verdict.

When Paul stood before King Agrippa, he told him about Christ's death, burial, and resurrection and his own conversion experience on the road to Damascus. When he was through, Agrippa said, "Almost thou persuadest me to be a Christian." Paul replied that he wished Agrippa and all who heard him that day "were both almost and altogether" persuaded (Acts 26:28-29).

That's preaching at its best. Paul was not pleading for his own life; he was pleading for the soul of Agrippa and all who heard his message that day.

All good preaching is like that. While preaching contains an element of teaching, our primary goal is a decision, a verdict, a commitment to Christ.

People are hungry for God's Word like I have never seen them before. When it is preached simply, clearly, and with authority and enthusiasm, people will come to hear it and churches will grow.

6
Flake Was No Fluke

If you want to build a growing church, magnify the Sunday School. It is the best tool we have for doing a lasting work for God.

Several years ago a newspaper carried the story of three hundred whales that died. The whales were pursuing sardines when they found themselves marooned in a bay and consequently they died. Frederick Brown Harris commented on this by saying, "The small fish lured the sea giants to their deaths. They came to the violent demise by chasing small ends, by prostituting their vast powers for insignificant goals."

Many churches are running the same risk. They are putting their greatest energies into small endeavors, and they are not giving the Sunday School priority.

The Sunday School is not just another organization of the church. It is the church organized and functioning to carry out the Great Commission. The Sunday School is the church meeting, maturing, ministering, and marching for the Master. It is the best possible organization for outreach, discipleship, ministry, and fellowship. We must, therefore, give our highest and best energies to building a strong Sunday School if we want to have a growing church.

There are, I believe, seven factors in Sunday School growth. They are:

(1) Anticipation—know your possibilities.

(2) Multiplication—enlarge the structure to meet your needs.

(3) Motivation—enlist the workers.

(4) Preparation—train the workers.

(5) Allocation—provide the space.

(6) Visitation—go after the people.

(7) Conservation—hang onto the results.

Let's look at these growth factors for a few minutes.

Anticipation—Know Your Possibilities

The best leadership is always built upon anticipation rather than reaction. Therefore, you should take a careful look at your field to see the possibilities that are there. The danger we all face is that of living so close to a situation that we become oblivious to the obvious.

My church is located a few blocks from two major hospitals. I drive to them several times every week. Sometimes, when I arrive at the hospital, I realize that I have seen nothing along the way. While I was driving down the street, my mind was somewhere else. I have driven that street so often that I have become oblivious to the things along the way. We are sometimes that way with our church fields.

Many churches need to restudy their field and rediscover their own possibilities. We need to open our eyes, take a census, or conduct a prospect search in order to see the possibilities that are around us. The French have a proverb that says, "What is seen is important. What is not seen is essential."

Two years ago we took a fresh look at our church field and saw a vast number of single adults who were not being reached by any church. Those people represented a vast potential for our Lord. We had had a small Single Adult ministry for years, but it had not grown significantly. So we decided to take the business approach. What was that? Business people do not sit around and wait until they are flooded with orders from an area before they place a sales representative there. Usually they see the potential of an area, hire a sale representative, and tell him to build the territory.

That's what we did. We called a minister of single adults and set him to work. The result is that we have developed one of the largest and finest Single Adult ministries anywhere. In two years, we have grown to five Single Adult departments, and we are still growing.

Do you need a Single Adult ministry in your area? Are vast numbers of young people not being reached? Are the elderly being cared for properly? Are minority groups being ministered to? What about the deaf, the handicapped, or special education children? Open your eyes, check your rolls, take a census, talk to the people in your community, visit the local school administrators. Discover the needs in your area, and start meeting them. That's the first step to Sunday School growth.

Multiplication — Enlarge Your Organization

The genius of Sunday School is in two things: its curriculum and its structure. The curriculum is the Bible. The structure is the small classroom unit organized on an age-group basis.

Two fundamental laws of Sunday School growth are: multiply by dividing and new units grow faster than established ones. So, we must keep creating new units in order to grow, and we must keep a good ratio between teachers and pupils. The ratio ought to be about one teacher to every ten pupils.

The Sunday School needs to be constantly expanding

and upgraded for its greatest efficiency. Organization is not an idol to be worshiped. It is a tool to be used. So, we must not hesitate to change it to make it more efficient.

When Arthur Flake once suggested the need for more organization to a certain church, the pastor protested saying, "We are too organized already. What we need is less organizing and more agonizing."

Flake replied, "Try organizing your Sunday School, and you'll have all the agonizing you can handle."

Teachers sometimes become too possessive of their positions, their classroom, and their pupils. They do not want to be moved or their pupils to be promoted. We must help them to see that the cause is more important than the organization. Reaching and teaching people is more important than having their own way.

I think it is safe to say that if we were to add no new space and create no new units we would strangle the growth of our Sunday School.

Motivation — Enlist Your Workers

The effectiveness of the Sunday School never rises above the ability, dedication, and work of the teachers who lead the classes. We must, therefore, magnify the office of teacher. We must help our people to realize that they are expected to grow to the point where they are able to teach God's word to others (Heb. 5:12) and help them to see that it is a tremendous honor and a signal responsibility to be a teacher (Jas. 3:1-2). About the only Bible study most people get during the week is what they get in Sunday School on Sunday morning. That makes teaching both sacred and serious.

Fred Smith, a management consultant, who takes hold of sick businesses and puts them on their feet again said,

"The difference between a good organization and a bad organization is structure. The difference between a good organization and a great organization is motivation." We must motivate our people to give their highest and their best to teaching God's word.

Preparation – Train Your Workers

It takes more than a baptismal certificate to make a good teacher. That's why, as I explain in chapter 9, we give teacher preparation prime time in our midweek program. In addition to our weekly meetings, we also have special training classes throughout the year.

If teachers think they do not need training, that very attitude disqualifies them for being good teachers. Unteachable teachers will be ineffective teachers. Arnold Glassow said, "Conceit is the quicksand of success." The moment teachers become overconfident, they become ineffective.

The road to good teaching is always under construction. Teddy Roosevelt used to say, "The man who thinks he has arrived is already on the return trip."

When people come to Sunday School, they want to hear God's Word. I visited with a lady in the hospital who was a converted Jew from Holland. In broken English, she questioned me about the program of our church. Then she said, "We used to go to church but we quit when they started sending my children letters saying, 'Come to Sunday School and get a goldfish' and 'Come to Sunday School and see Bozo the Clown.' I want my children to go to Sunday School to hear the Word of God, not for goldfish or for clowns."

That's what most people want and what everyone needs when they come to Sunday School. Teachers must be prepared to share God's Word with them effectively.

Allocation – Provide the Space

People must have a place to meet. Don't let your building limit your growth. Churches can do anything that they need to do, including providing the space to teach God's Word. If for some reason you can't provide all the space you need immediately, you can always improvise temporarily. We have had classes meeting in the gymnasium, bowling alley, game room, offices, vacant houses, and in the "Weight Watchers Building" located in a nearby shopping center. We are now seriously considering going to two Sunday Schools in order to double our space.

Visitation – Go After the People

Nothing produces more growth than a personal, systematic, and continuous visitation program. If you don't believe visitation works, go to the nearest international airport. There you will find thousands of sales representatives flying from coast to coast every day. They are going to make personal contacts on behalf of their businesses. Business people know that personal visits pay off.

My own conversion is a testimony to the effectiveness of visitation. I grew up in an apartment house in downtown Port Arthur, Texas. I was right across the alley from one church and half a block from another. But I never visited those churches. When I was in my early teens, a schoolmate took a personal interest in me and began to invite me to go to Sunday School. When I didn't respond, he started coming by my house on Sunday morning to take me with him. If I were awake, my mother would make me go. If I were still in bed, she would excuse me. I spent some of the most miserable hours of my life trying to stay in bed past 9:30 so I wouldn't have to go to Sunday School. But my friend persisted. He came again and again until finally I went with him. After a few months, I became a Christian and began attending on my own. It was visitation that led to my salvation.

I'm glad my friend cared about me when I didn't care about myself. He could have said, "He knows where the church is; let him come if he wants to." Or he could have said, "He doesn't care about himself; why should I care about him?" But because the concern inside the church exceeded the indifference on the outside of the church, a wonderful thing happened to me. There is a lesson here for all of us. We can't be indifferent to the indifference of others. We are to care for them even when they do not care about themselves.

Dennis Parrott, our minister of education, once asked our Sunday School teachers, "Is it true or false that when we go, they come?" They responded, "It's true. When we go, they come."

Then he asked, "Are you sure? Isn't it true that sometimes when we go they don't come?" This created second thoughts. Then one of the teachers said, "No, it is not true that when we go they come. But it is true that when we go, go, go, they come." That's the secret to visitation. We must go and keep on going.

There is no substitute for personal contacts. A recent issue of *Sports Illustrated* told how Barry Switzer recruited Billy Sims (later a Heisman Trophy winner) for the University of Oklahoma. When Coach Switzer decided he wanted Billy at Oklahoma, he first visited with him and then invited Billy to visit the O.U. campus. Then Switzer began phoning Billy every Saturday morning.

One Saturday afternoon Oklahoma was ahead of Colorado by about thirty points at the half, so Coach

Switzer had nothing to say to his team. He decided instead to call Billy and talk to him. He explained his persistency by saying, "I knew that if he was talking to me he couldn't be talking to anybody else." The fact of the matter is that the world puts us to shame with their recruiting.

If we were as concerned about enlisting people for Christ, we would see a better response.

The Sunday School is the best organization in the church for outreach and evangelism. It took me a long time to realize that. For many years in my ministry I kept trying to create new organizations for outreach. Usually by the time I got the organization formed and trained, I was exhausted and had lost interest. Then one day I realized that we already had the best organization possible for outreach: the Sunday School. All I needed to do was to activate it. That's when our church started to grow.

Conservation — Hang onto the Results

It is not enough to reach people. We must keep them and help them to grow to full maturity in Christ. We do this by teaching, fellowship, ministry, and visitation. Without a good program, we will find people coming in the front door and going right out the back door of the church.

Without a doubt, the Sunday School is the greatest discipling organization in the world. When you consider the number of people involved, the number of hours spent in study, and the overall impact of the Sunday School, nothing else can rival it. Why start something else, when with a little effort you can shape up the organization you already have?

Fifty years ago Arthur Flake, a great Sunday School leader, said essentially the same thing about how to build a Sunday School: "We must know our possibilities; enlarge the organization; provide the space; enlist and train the workers; and go after the people."

We are learning today that Flake was no fluke. He knew what he was talking about. In fact, J. N. Foreman, a former chaplain at the Texas Department of Corrections in Huntsville, told me that he had used these same principles to build an effective Sunday School inside the prison. (It occurs to me that he did have one advantage over most of us—his prospects were always in).

These are the basic laws of Sunday School growth. We must not neglect them or deviate from them. We must not become so sophisticated and educated that we think we can abandon them. If you want your church to grow, give priority to your Sunday School and begin implementing these principles immediately.

7
Do the Work of an Evangelist

For a church to grow, it must be evangelistic. You can't have an evangelistic church without an evangelistic pastor. If the pastor's heart burns hot for the lost, the whole church will soon be warmed. If the pastor is cold and indifferent, the church will soon suffer from spiritual frostbite.

That's why the apostle Paul said to Timothy, a pastor, "Do the work of an evangelist" (2 Tim. 4:5). An evangelist is "one who brings good news." In the original language, the word "evangelist" is not preceded by the definite article "an." When that is the case, character, quality, and nature are stressed. The idea is "let your work be evangelistic in nature." Paul was telling Timothy to always be a bringer of good news, to be ever reaching for souls in his preaching and teaching ministry. Paul was not exhorting local pastors to engage in an itinerant ministry of going from place to place holding evangelistic crusades. That work is especially for those gifted people called evangelists (Eph. 4:11). The local pastor should be evangelistic in message and method. Pastors should ever be reaching out for the lost in teaching, preaching, and personal contact.

Whenever the church grows, it has the kind of pastor who keeps reaching out after the lost. What does it mean for a pastor to do the work of an evangelist? How is this solemn charge carried out? It can be done in three ways: by public proclamation, by personal visitation, and by lay participation.

Public Proclamation

If you want to do the work of an evangelist, you should give attention to your preaching. The Bible says that "it pleased God by the foolishness of preaching to save them that believe" (1 Cor. 1:21). Jesus said, "I, if I be lifted up from the earth, will draw all men unto me" (John 12:32). The crucifixion and the proclamation of Christ have a universal and irresistible appeal. If you want to win people to Christ, you must preach the good news to them.

So, pastor, tell people that Christ died for their sins. Tell them that he was buried and on the third day he rose again. Tell them that he can give them forgiveness, life, hope, and salvation. Tell them about Christ. Don't preach beautiful ideas, preach Christ! Don't preach philosophy, preach Christ! Don't preach morals, preach Christ! Don't preach sermons, preach Christ!

When you have finished preaching, always give a clear and bold appeal for people to trust in Christ. The Bible closes with the great invitation, "And whosoever will, let him take the water of life freely" (Rev. 22:17).

The Spirit does not say, "Whosoever weeps may come." And he does not say, "Whosoever understands all things may come." And he does not say, "Whosoever is sure he can hold out may come." What he says is, "Whosoever will—wants to—may come." That's our appeal also. Look people in the eye, extend your arms to them, and from the depths of your heart ask them to come to the Savior. If you will do that, lost people will be saved.

But remember also that evangelism is not the exclusive work of the church. Robert Rains expressed it graphically: "The church is both evangelist and educator, both obstetrician and pediatrician, helping to deliver those newly born in Christ and nurturing them from infancy to maturity in

Christ." For that reason, very few of my sermons are evangelistic in nature. I preach primarily to Christians on Sunday and Wednesday. I always close my sermons with an evangelistic appeal. I always give an invitation. But 95 percent of the time, I feed the sheep on Sunday and do evangelism during the week.

Personal Visitation

Preaching is important. But it takes more than preaching to do the work of an evangelist. It also takes personal visitation. The apostle Paul used both methods and so must we (Acts 20:20).

You don't build a growing church by sitting around playing solitaire with the prospect cards. You do it by wearing out shoe leather and automobile tires in personal visitation.

J. D. Grey, former pastor of the First Baptist Church of New Orleans, Louisiana, once said that preachers ought to wear out their clothes in three places: on their knees, in fellowship with God; on their elbows, in fellowship with the great minds of the ages; and on the soles of their shoes, in fellowship with God's people.

McDonald Goppe, a West Indian evangelist, characterized his ministry by saying, "I have the head of a Baptist, the heart of a Pentecostal, and the feet of a Jehovah's Witness." That's a hard combination to beat.

The Bible speaks interestingly about the preacher's feet. "How beautiful are the feet of them that preach the gospel of peace, and bring glad tidings of good things!" (Rom. 10:15). That was a strange verse of Scripture to me for many years. I couldn't understand it. I had never thought of people's feet as being beautiful. Useful, yes! But beautiful? No!

I've known people who have had a beautiful shape,

beautiful eyes, beautiful legs, beautiful lips, beautiful hair, and even beautiful hands. But I have never known of anyone who had beautiful feet.

Why did the writer call preachers' feet beautiful? It was because feet are instruments of divine appointment. They are the primary means of transportation. It was by the use of the feet that the messenger delivered his message. So, in a real sense if the feet do not go the message does not go. Missions and evangelism reduced to their lowest common denominator get down to feet.

One Way to Do It

I am sometimes asked to explain the outreach program of our church and my part in it. Our program is simple but comprehensive. We begin by visiting newcomers. When the church was smaller, I did most of this myself. Now that the church is larger it is done by an associate.

After people visit our morning services, my associate and I telephone them that same afternoon. This is an invaluable contact. People are impressed that I take time to call them so quickly. From these calls, we learn where the visitors are from, what their occupations are, about their families, how they happened to visit our church, and what their spiritual status is.

On the basis of the information gained from the visitors' cards and the telephone conversations, visitation assignments are then made to staff members, Sunday School classes, and deacons. Everyone on our staff visits. The associate pastor makes assignments and reports are given at our weekly staff meetings. As the pastor, I'm actively involved in the visitation program. I try to make a minimum of five prospect visits a week. in other pastorates when I had fewer administrative and counseling responsibilities, I made as many as ten visits a week.

Like any pastor, I have to fight for every minute of visitation time I have. I concentrate primarily on families and on men. Two things have proven most helpful to me. First, I visit every Wednesday night after prayer meeting. I allow almost nothing to interfere with this visitation time. Not even the weather. In fact, I have discovered that the worse the weather is the more likely I am to catch prospects at home. It rarely snows in Tyler, but two years ago on a snowy afternoon I went out visiting. When I arrived at a prospect's house, he was playing in the snow with his little boy. When he saw me, he asked in surprise, "What are you doing out in weather like this?" I replied, "I'm out because you are in."

I can usually make at least two visits on Wednesday night. Sometimes I will take a deacon, a young person, or some other lay person with me.

Second, the church gives me an expense allowance so I can take prospects to lunch. I do this several times each week. It is easy to get together with men at this time, and it gives me an hour of uninterrupted time with them. There is not television blaring, no phone calls, and no children crying. This is probably the most productive visitation time I have. Sometimes I will make a visit or two on my way home from the office or on my way to a meeting.

When I'm away in a revival meeting or a mission trip or on some special occasion, I write prospects a postcard and let them know I'm praying for them and that our church is still interested in them. I have my secretary preaddress and stamp these cards before I leave. That way all I have to do is jot a quick note on the card and mail it. I usually do this on the plane or my first night in a motel.

I rank the writing of cards as one of my most effective

tools for reaching people. People are impressed that I remember them and take time to write them. Twice in the last two weeks people have told me how much my cards have meant to them.

I feel that it is imperative for me to be actively engaged in prospect visitation for several reasons.

(1) Because of my position and experience, I am the most effective visitor for the church.

(2) I must do this to fulfill my calling (Acts 20:20).

(3) It adds to my own spiritual enrichment. I preach better on Sunday if I have been out visiting during the week.

(4) I must set an example if I'm going to motivate others to visitation.

Lay Participation

I believe not only in the priesthood of the believer but also in the preacherhood of the believer. I believe that every Christian ought to be a witness for Christ. If we are to do the work of an evangelist, we must enlist, motivate, and train our lay people to share their faith effectively.

Every great evangelist has done this. John the Baptist was an evangelist. When he conducted city-wide crusades, merchants closed their shops and the people emptied the streets to hear him preach. But John did more than thunder out repentance. He also equipped lay people. How do I know? Because the disciples came to Jesus and said to him, "Lord, teach us to pray as John taught his disciples" (Luke 11:1).

Jesus was also an evangelist. He preached to the great multitudes, and he also went to the homes of people like Zacchaeus to bring them to salvation. However, he spent most of his time teaching, training, and equipping his twelve apostles. Mark tells us that he called them to be "with him" (Mark 3:14).

When Jesus saw the multitudes, he said to his disciples, "The fields are ripe unto harvest, and the laborers are few. Pray that the Lord of harvest will send forth laborers into the harvest." Then he gave those same disciples instructions and power and sent them out to witness two by two (Luke 9:1-2). Later, he enlisted, trained, and sent out another seventy on a similar assignment (Luke 10:1-16).

Paul was an evangelist. He honeycombed the Roman Empire with new churches that he established. Wherever he went, he started either a revival or a riot. But he also spent much time in training others to do God's work.

He said to Timothy, "The things which thou hast heard of me . . . the same commit thou to faithful men, who shall be able to teach others also" (2 Tim. 2:2).

It takes more to witness than a mouth. Lay people need to know what to say. They need to know how to make an approach. They need to be able to answer questions. And they need to have the right spirit. It is our responsibility to train them, equip them, for this task.

For every minister who has the courage to tackle it, there is a full-time job in the raising and training of a battalion of Christian workers who will become gospel nets to drag their communities and to catch people for God.

Pastor, you need not be in a big place to do a big work for God. Be faithful and true and diligent in your ministry where you are and God will bless you. I charge you, therefore, before God and the Lord Jesus Christ, who will judge the living and the dead at his appearing: Do the work of an evangelist. Do it where you are. Do it day in and day out. Do it with all of your strength. Ever and always be at the task of bringing men and women to Christ, and your church will grow.

8

The Pastor and People Working Together

On a recent mission trip to Brazil, I visited a number of churches along the banks of the Amazon River, deep in the heart of the Amazon Valley. One of those churches was named "The Always Alive Baptist Church."

One of the unusual things about this church, besides its name, was the fact that it was celebrating its seventieth anniversary that year and it had never had a pastor. When I heard that, it occurred to me that that might be one of the reasons why this church was "always alive." Most churches are entirely too pastor-centered. Not nearly enough emphasis is given to the role and the responsibilities of lay people in doing the work of the Lord.

The really growing churches are those where the pastor and people do God's word together. The office of pastor is from God. The apostle Paul made this clear when he wrote:

He [God] gave some, apostles; and some, prophets; and some, evangelists; and some, pastors and teachers; For the perfecting of the saints, for the work of the ministry, for the edifying of the body of Christ: Till we all come in the unity of the faith, and of the knowledge of the Son of God, unto a perfect man, unto the measure of the stature of the fulness of Christ (Eph. 4:11-13).

The apostles were the original twelve who accompanied Jesus during his earthly ministry. The prophets were inspired preachers of the word of God. Evangelists were itinerant preachers who traveled from place to place establishing churches. They were the rank and file missionaries of their day. The pastor-teachers were leaders of local congregations. The word *pastor* means "shepherd." It refers to one who watches over the flock, feeds it, and tends to its every need.

These verses help us to see how the pastor and his people are to work together in ministering for God. They speak to us of the shepherd's fold, the shepherd's role, and the shepherd's goal.

The Shepherd's Fold

Paul identified the shepherd's fold as "the saints." The Scriptures give five names to Christians: believers, for their faith; brethren, for their love; disciples, for their knowledge; servants for their work; and saints, for their holiness.

The word *saint* literally means "one who is set apart." Christians then are the people of God who have been set apart for his holy service.

Two little boys were talking after church one Sunday and one asked the other, "What is a saint?"

The second little boy was not altogether sure. But he did remember that the stained-glass windows in the sanctuary of his church had representations of the twelve apostles in them. He remembered sitting in church and seeing the soft sunlight filter through those stained glass images. He said to his friend, "I'm not sure, but I think a saint is a person who lets the light shine through."

Not bad. All Christians are saints. Our mission in life is to let the light of Jesus shine through our lives. We do this best as we minister for him. When Jesus saved us, he saved us from something and to something and for something. He saves us from sin, to life, and for service.

The Lord did not save us to sit, soak, and sour. He saved us to serve. It's high time that more of God's people rolled up their sleeves and got involved in the work of the ministry and the edifying of the body of Christ. We are his sheep. We make up the shepherd's fold.

The Shepherd's Role

What is the role of the shepherd in relationship to the fold? It is to "perfect" the saints. The word *perfect* is a fisherman's term. It means to "mend a net" to make it fit for use. When you fish with a net, there is always a danger of snagging it on something and tearing holes in it. A torn net will not function properly. The tear allows the fish to escape. So, a fisherman's net must occasionally be mended to make it fit for action.

This is the role of pastors. By teaching, preaching, training, and example, they are to equip church members for God's service. Pastors are to ready Christians for action and to make them useful in the kingdom's service. It is not the pastors' job to meet every need of their congregations. It is their job to see that every need is met.

Both churches and pastors need to understand this concept of the pastor. Many do not see this as the primary role. Several years ago, in another church, I was encouraging my deacons to get involved in visitation and ministry to other people. It was evident as I spoke that my words were falling on deaf ears. When I finished, one of the elderly deacons who had been practicing what I was talking about spoke up. He said, "Men, we must help our pastor to do his work."

His words stunned me. While I greatly appreciated the spirit in which they were spoken, he had missed the very point I was trying to make. So, I thanked him and told my deacons, "It is not your responsibility to help me do my work. It is my responsibility to help you do God's work." The work is his. The church is his. We are his. It is not my responsibility to do all of the work of the Lord by myself. It is my responsibility to enlist, to train, and to motivate his lay people to become involved in his service.

Many pastors fail most miserably at this point. I had just finished speaking on this subject in an associational meeting when the pastor of the church where we were meeting came over to sit beside me. He said, "Paul, this is personal confession time. I have been the pastor of this church for fifteen years, and I cannot look out across the congregation and find one layman whom I have trained to witness for Christ." What a tragedy! Both pastors and people must accept this biblical concept of the ministry if our churches are going to grow.

The Shepherd's Goal

To what end is the shepherd to perfect the saints? There are two goals: unto the work of the ministry and unto the edifying of the body of Christ.

The first responsibility of the pastor is to prepare people to minister for Christ. Involvement is the life-blood of the church. We must constantly be presenting people with opportunities to get involved directly in ministry, mission, and evangelism. The church staff alone is not to do all the work of the ministry. Lay people should be visiting in the hospitals, ministering in retirement homes, calling on shut-ins, and comforting the brokenhearted.

The word *minister* in the Greek is the same word that is oftentimes translated "deacon." Pastors are to train people to do a deacon's kind of work. What is a deacon's kind of work? The office of deacon is greatly misunderstood by most people today. They think of the deacons as a board of directors who run the church. They believe that they are to meet once a month to review the finances of the church and make recommendations to the business meetings. In many churches that is about all they do.

This is the lowest concept of a deacon there is. The first deacons were elected to deliver groceries (Acts 6:1-6). They were special servants of Christ and his church to meet the practical needs of widows. The office of deacon achieves its highest honor when it leads to that kind of service. As deacons fulfill their high calling, they free the pastor to pray and preach as God intended.

Too many churches have adopted the world's standards. They measure greatness in terms of authority, power, and rule. That's why they are in trouble. Have you ever noticed that most of the trouble in churches results from little people wanting to rule, not from big people wanting to serve?

It is the deacons' service and ministry that actually qualifies them to make business decisions. The business of the church can never be determined on the basis of dollars and cents alone. Unless deacons are out among the people, feeling their pain and heartache, deacons can't know how best to spend the Lord's money, what new staff members are needed, and what new programs ought to be inaugurated. For deacons to make business decisions without first being among the people in ministry is like a doctor trying to treat a patient he has never seen. A physician needs to feel the patient's pulse, look into the patient's eyes, and check his temperature to treat him effectively. It takes personal contact with the patient to prescribe the best cure. The same thing is true with spiritual healing.

In our church, we expect all of our deacons to minister in some special capacity. We do not get 100 percent participation, of course, and that doesn't bother me. I keep in mind that many of our deacons were ordained without any expectations beyond attending a monthly meeting. No one taught them in advance about ministry. So, they have served for many years with no other expectations. For me to suddenly put new demands on them is unfair. However, all of the new deacons we ordain are taught to minister. Their decision to be ordained as deacons is a decision to become ministers. And a decision to quit ministering is a decision to no longer be a deacon. A nonministering deacon is a contradiction of terms. So, our deacons lead the way in ministry in our church.

Nine Ways to Minister

We have nine different ministries that our deacons are involved in. Each year I ask our deacons to volunteer for one of these and to stay with it all year.

These areas of ministry are:

1. Hospital vistitation. A different deacon visits the hospitals each day of the week. The deacon calls the church office to get the names of our people who are sick and then visits the hospital at his convenience. In the last four years, one of our men has made over 1200 visits in the hospital. He has kept a record of the names of all the people he has visited, and he finds great joy in remembering his time with them.

Think of the joy he would have missed and the joy our people would have missed if we hadn't had this ministry. As a result of these faithful deacons, our church enjoys a reputation of caring for its people. As a hospital chaplain said recently, "We can always tell when people are members of

Green Acres because they are visited so effectively."

2. Rest home chaplain. A deacon is assigned as the chaplain of each of the six rest homes in our community. They visit every member of our church, and anyone else in their rest home who needs help. They visit once a week and try to be sensitive to the needs of people around them and notify the church of these special needs.

3. Shut-in visitation. All of our shut-ins have a deacon assigned to them. The deacon visits them once a week and ministers to them. One of our men bought his shut-in a radio so she could listen to the broadcast of our worship services. He and his wife had her in their home periodically for dinner. When she was in the hospital, they tended to her in a special way. They were the only family she had. When we buried her recently, this faithful deacon was one of her pallbearers. He is now ready for another assignment.

4. Spiritual gifts. The men in this ministry visit each person who joins our church and encourages them to discover what their spiritual gift is and begin using it for Christ.

5. Fellowship ministry. After each worship service, I invite our visitors to a reception in my study. Deacons serve coffee, greet the visitors, and then later assist them in finding their way around our buildings. They also direct a monthly fellowship for new members which is held in the pastor's home on Sunday night following one of the evening worship services. At this fellowship, we ask each new member to give some personal information and the reason(s) for joining Green Acres. Having these events in the pastor's study and the pastor's home adds a personal touch that the people greatly appreciate.

6. Crisis ministry. These deacons minister to people who are going through times of crisis, such as a terminal illness, a divorce, or a death.

7. Evangelism and outreach. This is a group of specially trained deacons who visit prospects each week. Once a prospect is assigned to them, they are to keep that prospect on their prayer list and visitation list and continue to follow up until that person makes some decision.

8. Prayer ministry. These deacons help promote the ministry of prayer in our church, especially on Wednesday nights. They sit at assigned tables and lead out in the prayer time during our midweek services. They also build attendance at prayer meeting by inviting new members to join them for the Wednesday evening services.

9. Discipleship ministry. These men teach special classes, lead monthly discipleship retreats, and work one-on-one to disciple people.

In addition to these special ministries, there are countless other ways our people can get involved in practical ministry to others.

Many people, when they describe their church, say, "Our church has one minister and five-hundred members." What they ought to say is, "Our church has one pastor and five-hundred ministers." All of God's people are to be ministers, and it is the pastor's responsibility to equip them for special service.

Be a Body Builder

The pastor is also to equip lay people to "edify" the body of Christ. The word *edify* is a construction term. From it we get the word *edifice*. It means to build up, to construct. It is the role of the plain vanilla Christian to build up the body of Christ. He is to help build it both bigger and stronger. There is a difference between muscle and fat. Some churches are getting bigger but they aren't getting stronger. Every Christian has a responsibility to help the church grow both numerically and spiritually.

It is not the responsibility of the preacher to fill the pews. His responsibility is to fill the pulpit. The members are to fill the pews.

When many Christians and pastors think of getting the lay people involved in the church, they think only in terms of serving on committees. Serving on a committee is not the same as ministering. The modern church is much like an army that puts all of its privates on committees to make battle plans and sends only the generals out to fight the war. While the generals are suffering from battle fatigue, the foot soldiers are sitting in tents sipping coffee and evaulating the progress of the war. Our churches are losing the war against sin and Satan today, not because the enemy has superior forces or because our weapons are inadequate or because we have no ammunition, but because our soldiers are not fighting. Our need is for more foot-soldiers, not more advisers.

Neither the pastor nor the lay people should equate attending meetings with practical ministry.

This then is the shepherd's fold, the shepherd's role, and the shepherd's goal. Pastors are to stay at this task until all Christians come to full maturity in Jesus Christ. What does it mean to be like him? Jesus was first and foremost a servant. He came not to be ministered unto, but to minister. We are to grow to the place where we are ready to serve other people and the Heavenly Father as Jesus did.

The goal of the Christian life is not just to escape hell and go to heaven. The goal of the Christian life is to become like Jesus Christ. He is our model, our example, our goal. We are to keep growing until we become like him.

9
The Midweek Power Hour

Do I need to sell you on the importance of prayer? Surely not. Prayer is the mightiest force in all the world. Prayer can empower a preacher. Prayer can revive a church. Prayer can heal the sick. Prayer can save a soul. Prayer can change a life. It is because Jesus knew the tremendous power of prayer that he said, "Men ought always to pray, and not to faint" (Luke 18:1). That word *ought* suggests moral imperative. Prayer is a matchless privilege. We all know that. But it is more than just a privilege. It is also a duty.

For whom should we pray?

The Scope of Prayer

We are taught to pray for the sick (Jas. 5:14). I'm often asked, "Do you believe in faith healing?" I most assuredly do. The day of miracles is not past. With God all things are possible. But I do not believe in faith healers. There is a big difference. James committed the ministry of prayer for the sick to the local church and not to traveling tent evangelists or electronic church healers.

We ought to pray for little children (Matt. 19:13). The older I grow the more I love little children. I like to encourage them. I enjoy speaking to them. And I want to pray for them. I realize more and more that the making and unmaking of the world is in little children. Their character is formed and set so very early. Jesus prayed for little children, and we should also.

We ought to pray for our leaders (1 Tim. 2:1-4). This is our best hope for peace and godliness in the world. Through prayer for our leaders, I can affect the world in which I live. I doubt if I'll ever be invited to the White House to advise the president. If I wrote him a letter, he would probably never read it. But I can do something more than advise him face-to-face or through the mail. I can pray for him, and there is no way anyone can keep my prayers from penetrating the wall of separation built around him. Through prayer, I can lift him to God and help create in him a hunger and thirst after the counsel of the Lord.

We ought to pray for laborers. Matthew tells us that as Jesus moved among the multitudes he was moved by them. He saw them as defeated and whipped down by the circumstances of life. Their lives were shattered, fractured, with no integrating center. They were like sheep without a shepherd. There was nothing to hold their lives together. It was then that Jesus said to pray to the Lord of harvest and ask him to send forth laborers into the harvest (Matt. 9:36-38).

Everywhere missionaries, pastors, staff members, and Sunday School teachers are in short supply. The answer to an adequate labor force in the church is prayer. We are to pray that the Lord will "send forth" laborers. The word *send* is a very strong word in the Greek. It means to "drive out" or to "thrust out." It is the same word Jesus used when he cast the demons out of a man. It is the same word that was used to describe what Jesus did when he drove the money changers out of the Temple. We are to pray that the Lord of harvest will send such an irresistible compulsion upon the hearts of people that they will be thrust out into the work of the Lord. The church that is not producing laborers is failing, regardless of what else it may be doing.

We ought to pray for our enemies (Matt. 5:43-45). There are two ways to get rid of our enemies. We can destroy them or we can make friends with them. Through prayer for our enemies, we grow to love them as Jesus loved those who crucified him.

We are to pray for the lost (Rom. 10:1). We must never forget why the church is here. It exists to win the lost to Christ and to help Christians mature in their faith. George Weber said, "Any church that does not recognize the basic purpose of its existence is in jeopardy of its life."

The predicament of the American church is precisely that it has lost sight of the fact that it is a missions situation.

There are 138,000 more lost people in the world today than there were yesterday. If all the lost in the world were lined up thirty inches apart they would encircle the globe not one time, not two times, not three times, but thirty times. That line is growing at a rate of twenty-five miles per day.

At the close of his earthly ministry, Jesus prayed and wept over the city of Jerusalem. Like a mother hen, he longed to draw that great city to the safety and security of his sheltering wings (Matt. 23:37-39).

Nothing so reveals the heartbeat of our Savior than this experience. It should be the heartbeat of all of God's people. As Jesus wept and prayed over his city, so ought we to weep and pray over ours.

We must pray that the whole gospel will be preached by the whole church to the whole world with our whole hearts.

Growing churches make much of prayer. If you want your church to grow, teach your people how to pray. John the Baptist and Jesus taught their people. Pray yourself. Bathe all your decisions in prayer. Set aside and call the people to days of prayer. Organize prayer groups. Form prayer chains. Above all, make prayer meeting a prayer meeting.

The Problem of Scheduling

Traditionally Wednesday night has been prayer meeting night in churches. However, prayer meeting has become the Cinderella of the church. It is unloved and unwooed by almost everyone. It ought to be the most exciting and meaningful service of the church. But it is not so. In the average church, Sunday morning services are a "blowout" and Wednesday night services ar a "bomb-out."

There are two basic problems we face with our Wednesday night programs: how to schedule all of the needed activities into a limited amount of time and how to get the people into a meaningful prayer experience.

Scheduling is of prime importance. We begin with a family meal served from 5:30-6:30. Then we have three activities running simultaneously from 6:30-7:30. We have Children's choir, Sunday School teachers' preparation time, and prayer meeting. These activities are followed by Adult choir rehearsal, committee meetings, and our all-church visitation.

This scheduling allows us to give prime time to our teacher preparation. We want to give this activity the best time possible because our Sunday School is so important to us. It also allows us to have our visitation time on Wednesday night. This is the best time for church visitation for several reasons:

(1) Wednesday night is traditionally recognized as church night and so our community does not schedule

many other activities then. This makes it easier to find prospects at home.

(2) Since our primary outreach thrust is through the Sunday School and our teachers are already present for their preparation time, it is easy to make assignments to them.

(3) Since the people are already at church, it saves them from another night of regular church activities. It is easy to make one or two visits to prospects or absentees on the way home from church.

We don't want our people coming to the church every night of the week. I don't even like to go to church that much myself. Going to church every night doesn't make me a better Christian. Frankly, it makes me worse.

A Meaningful Prayer Time

In our prayer meeting time, we strive for a genuine prayer experience. Through the years, I have probably killed more midweek services than any other preacher alive. I did it by trying to make prayer meeting a real prayer meeting.

I've always believed in and practiced private prayer. I also know that the church needs to pray together. But how do we get them to do it?

In my efforts, I tried everything. I tried silent prayer, voluntary prayer, calling on specific people for prayer, and breaking up into small prayer groups. But nothing worked. It seemed that people would come to prayer meeting for anything but prayer.

Then I discovered the secret of getting people into a meaningful prayer experience, and it has worked beautifully for three years. I decided to conduct our prayer services in our fellowship hall, around the same tables we use for our evening meal.

After a congregational hymn, I call our people to prayer. Using a printed prayer reminder that lists the names of our people who are sick, new members who have joined our church the previous Sunday, our missionaries who have had birthdays that week, our shut-ins, and other prayer requests, I remind our people of the pressing needs around us. A candle and a match have been placed on each table. I then ask each table to light its candle, and we turn the house lights out. The people at all the tables then pray simultaneously. This means that there are many little prayer meetings going on at once. Everyone is able to participate in the prayer time. The soft candlelight gives a sense of privacy and of sacredness.

A deacon is assigned to each table and is asked to direct the prayer and share time. Sometimes we begin by asking volunteers at each table to share their conversion experience, an experience of answered prayer, or a favorite verse of Scripture with the people at their table. Sometimes the people join hands around the table as they pray. Led by the deacon, the people at each table then pray around the circle. If a person does not wish to pray aloud for any reason, he simply says "amen" aloud and the prayer passes to the next person. When those at each table have finished praying, they blow out their candle. When all the candles are out we know that everyone is through praying, and we sing together the hymn "Sweet Hour of Prayer."

I then close our prayer time with a pastoral prayer.

Card to the Sick

When the lights are on again, we take two or three minutes to write postcards to the sick. Special prayer-postcards are placed on each table, along with several ballpoint pens. We encourage each person at the table to write to a different person who is sick and then have everyone at the table sign every card. In that way, all our sick receive cards that are signed by all of the people. The cards are left on the table and picked up later by a secretary to be mailed from the church office the next day. It is a great encouragement to the sick when they receive these cards and assurances of prayer in their behalf.

Scripture Memorization

We continue the services with more congregational singing. Several times during the year we devote five or ten minutes to Scripture memorization. Scriptures cards are printed and distributed among the people to help them in their memory work. They are printed on plain white sheets of paper, with dotted lines so they can be cut to card size for easier handling. The people can then carry them in their pockets or purses, pin them on their sun visor to memorize while driving, or tape them on their bathroom mirror and memorize them while they are getting ready for the day. Scriptures like Romans 3:23; 6:23; John 3:16; Romans 10:9-10; 13; Revelation 3:20, and Ephesians 2:8-9 are used. For a month after we have distributed the Scripture memory verses, we have a review time in our midweek services. Sometimes I call out the text and ask a volunteer to quote the verse. At other times, I quote the verse and ask a volunteer to tell me where it is found. Or I may ask questions like, "Why does a person need to be saved?" or "What must a person do to be saved?" and ask for a volunteer to respond by quoting a verse that answers that question. This is an effective way of reviewing the plan of salvation every week for a month.

Occasionally we memorize verses of Scripture by the alphabet. I will select and print two verses of Scripture that begin with each letter of the alphabet. For example, using the letter *A*, I select "All have sinned, and come short of the glory of God" (Rom. 3:13) and "All we like sheep have gone astray" (Isa. 53:6); I go through the entire alphabet arranging Scripture verses this way. I call out a letter of the alphabet and ask a volunteer to recite a verse that begins with that letter. This memory plan encompasses many subjects other than salvation.

Getting into the Bible

After the special music, I lead a thirty-minute Bible study. This is usually a verse-by-verse study of some book of the Bible. I do not make an effort to preach a sermon. The only structure I use is the outline of the Scripture passage as it comes from the Bible. A lot of emphasis is given to word study. This not only makes the Wednesday night study different from those of Sunday morning and Sunday night, but it also enriches the people's understanding of the Bible. These studies often become the basis for future sermons that will be preached on Sunday morning or Sunday night. Once I have taught a book on Wednesday night, it is much easier to go back through that book a couple of years later and develop structured sermons from my notes.

Two years ago we devoted six months to the study of the Book of Psalms. I asked the people to read one psalm every day for 150 days. Then each Wednesday night, I taught one of the seven psalms that they had read during the previous week. Until that time, the Book of Psalms had not meant very much to me. But as I dug into it for my Wednesday night studies, I discovered the gold mine that was there. Since that time I have preached sermons from Psalms again and again.

I followed the study in Psalms with a study of Proverbs. My study of Proverbs delighted and inspired me over and over again. Practical insight into everyday living kept leaping off the pages into my imagination and into my sermon preparation. Insights into family living, economics, politics, sexual behavior, and basic human relations were everywhere. Faith and common sense marched back and forth across the pages of the Proverbs. Answers for living are in this book of wisdom.

I asked our people to use Proverbs as their spiritual calendar and to read one chapter from Proverbs each day of the month. There are thirty-one chapters in Proverbs, so I asked them to read the chapter number that corresponded to each day of the month. On the first day of the month, they were to read chapter 1; on the second day they were to read chapter 2, and so forth. If a month had only thirty days in it, they were to read chapters 30 and 31 on the last day and then they would be back on schedule with their spiritual calendar.

Then each Wednesday night for thirty-one weeks I selected one proverb from each chapter as the basis of my message. Those who participated read the Book of Proverbs through once a month for over six months. What an enriching experience it was for all of us!

Sermons By the People

Sometimes in these studies I asked the people to help me develop a message. For example, when I came to the psalm that said, "I was glad when they said unto me, Let us go into the house of the Lord" (Ps. 122:1) I pointed out that church attendance ought to be a joyous experience. I then asked the people at each table to discuss and list the reasons church attendance was a glad experience for them. These discussions often led to a deep sharing from their own experiences. I then called on the deacon leader at each table to share one reason why church was a glad experience to the people at his table. One said, "We enjoy going to church because we hear the word of God preached"—that is the joy of learning. Another said, "We enjoy going to church because we get to sing great hymns"—that is the joy of praise. Another said, "We enjoy going to church because we meet our Christian friends there"—that is the joy of fellowship. After each group had responded I then summarized what the group had shared, and it became a very good sermon.

When I was teaching the Book of Proverbs, I often did the same thing. When I came to the proverb that said, "Death and life are in the power of the tongue" (Prov. 18:21), I asked the people at half of the tables to discuss and list some deadly uses of the tongue. I asked the people at the other half of the tables to discuss and list some constructive uses of it. When I asked the table leaders to share the deadly uses of the tongue, they mentioned such things as gossip, criticism, and profanity. When I asked for some good uses of the tongue they listed such things as encouragement, witnessing, and prayer.

Then I summarized the findings of the groups and the people left with a message impressed in their minds concerning the power of the tongue. I do not use this method often, but occasionally it adds variety and leads to group participation and the sharing of Christian experiences.

Growing churches don't just endure Wednesday night, they enjoy it. They turn it into a real power hour by making it a time of prayer, as well as a time of Bible study, preparation, and fellowship.

10
Christ, Children, and His Church

One day an artist was busy sketching a country landscape near a French village when a group of children gathered to watch him. Presently one of the little children approached him and asked, "Please, mister, sir, would you put us in the picture?"

If you want your church to grow, you must give children a prominent place in its picture.

Jesus and Little Children

This is the way it ought to be. Jesus loved little children and so should we. Mark, in his Gospel, tells us of some parents who brought their children to Jesus so he could bless them. The Greek word that Mark used for children tells us that these were probably not infants. These were probably children between the ages of four and twelve (Mark 10:13-16).

Jesus was on his way to Jerusalem, and the cross loomed heavily before him. His disciples, assuming that he had no time to be bothered with little children, tried to prevent these parents from bringing their children to Jesus. But Jesus did not share their feelings. What his disciples did displeased him very much. The word *displeased* is a very strong word in the Greek. It means to be "irritated" or "angered." Though his disciples' intentions were good, they did not understand Jesus at all. So, he told his disciples,

"Suffer the little children to come unto me, and forbid them not: for of such is the kingdom of God" (Mark 10:14).

Then, as he so often did, Jesus seized this opportunity to teach forceful truth about his kingdom. Using those little children as models, he said, "Verily I say unto you, Whosoever shall not receive the kingdom of God as a little child he shall not enter therein" (Mark 10:15). The words *shall not* in the Greek are a double negative. They literally mean "shall not never enter in." The use of a double negative is poor English, but it is excellent Greek. It is the strongest possible way of expressing a truth. Jesus was saying in the strongest possible language that unless we become like little children there is no way for us to enter into the kingdom of God.

The Attitude of Jesus

This experience is important for three reasons: first, it shows us the attitude of Jesus toward little children. The fact that he was angry at his disciples for hindering the little children from coming unto him shows how important children are to him. He wants children to come to him and he is angered when anyone hinders their coming.

When we know how Jesus feels about little children, how can we be indifferent to them ourselves? How can we ignore their religious questions? How can we brush aside their spiritual inquiries? How can we allow our children to grow up and be strangers to prayer? To the church? To the Bible? And to the plan of salvation?

Edith Shafer, commenting on our Lord's "woe" to those who offended children (Matt. 18:7) said, "A child is being robbed or 'offended' if he or she is not given the truth with enough explanation and answers to questions that there is a measure of understanding."

The Appeal of Jesus

The experience also shows us the appeal of Jesus. He is not only willing to receive little children but also he is anxious that they be brought to him. He said not to put obstacles in their way.

Many parents take a "hands-off" attitude toward the religious training and inquiries of their children. They say that they want to let the child decide for himself. But the world is unwilling to assume such a position of neutrality concerning our children, and we can't afford to take it either. The appeal of Jesus is simple. We are to bring our children to him. We are to teach them about him. We are to help them to know him and love him.

Eugene Chamberlain wrote in *When Can a Child Believe?* that there are two dangers relating to the salvation of children: (1) Too much too soon—pushing younger children to making decisions for which they are not prepared and (2) too little too late—neglecting older children who are mature enough to accept Christ. We must guard against both extremes.

Children can experience genuine salvation when they have reached the level of maturity at which they recognize their sins and come to Christ under the convicting power of the Holy Spirit.

Children should not be pushed away from Christ or pushed toward him. They should be given the opportunity to respond to him without pressure or hindrance from adults or other children.

Many children at a relatively early age can respond to Christ as Savior. Spurgeon said, "The capacity for believing lies more in the child than in the man. We grow less rather than more capable of faith."

Polycarp, one of the early martyrs of the church, was converted when he was nine years of age. All of his life he was faithful to Christ. As an old man, he was told he must renounce Christ or be put to death. He replied, "Eighty and six years have I served Christ; He has never done me any harm; then why should I deny His name?"

Isaac Watts, who wrote the marvelous hymn "When I Survey the Wondrous Cross" was converted when he was nine years old.

Jonathan Edwards, who led America in the Great Awakening by lighting revival fires all over our country, was converted when he was only seven years old.

Henry Ward Beecher, the great preacher who stirred all of New England with his powerful sermons, received his first religious impulse when he was but a lad of five.

Matthew Henry, author of one of our greatest Bible commentaries, was converted at eleven. And E. Stanley Jones, the great Methodist missionary to India, said that he was first moved to be a missionary when he was only seven years old. It has been true again and again that when children are brought to Jesus Christ, they trust him in a life-changing way.

Thus, Spurgeon wrote,

Ere your child has reached to seven
Teach him well the way to heaven.
And better still the work will thrive
If you'll teach him before he is five.

The Application of Jesus

Jesus made an application from this experience. He used those little children as models of the kingdom of heaven. He said that unless we receive the kingdom of God as little children we cannot enter therein. This is the very opposite of our thinking. We want little children to come to Jesus like adults. Jesus wants adults to come to him like little children. We have the whole process reversed.

What is there about little children that makes them models of the kingdom of God? First, there is their humility. Children are so unassuming. Nothing characterizes them like humility. We must have the humility of a little child if we are to be saved. Nobody struts into the kingdom of God.

Second, little children are honest. They have not yet learned to cover up, to put on a facade, to pretend, like adults do. If you ask little children questions, they will tell you exaclty what they think. There is no pretense, no hypocrisy, about them.

Finally, their faith makes them models. It is the nature of a little child to believe, to trust. In fact, when children are small they are so trusting you must teach them not to get into cars with strangers.

A little child believes that his parents know and can do anything. Children don't worry about inflation, the energy crisis, or international affairs. They believe that whatever is wrong with the world their parents can fix.

We must have that kind of faith in God to be saved. We do not come to God as Ph.Ds. We come to him as little children.

Because little children mean so much to Jesus, they must mean much to us. Jesus loves the little children, and we should love them and take time for them also.

The Pastor and Little Children

As a pastor, I pay attention to children. When I meet them in the halls, I speak to them. When I am greeting the congregation at the close of our services, I not only shake hands with adults but also I stop and stoop down to speak to the children. When they write me notes or draw me pictures, I always write them a thank-you note.

I keep a jar of hard candy in my study at all times. Before and after Sunday School, many of the children stop by to get a piece of candy. This gives me an opportunity to speak to them and to know them better. This is my method, even though it may not be yours.

At the close of our Sunday evening services, I usually ask all of the children to come forward for an informal chat. I take a hand mike, sit on the steps of our platform, and they gather around me on the floor. I then interview those who have had birthdays that week. I ask them questions like: "What is your name? When was your birthday? How old are you? What grade are you in? What is your favorite subject in school? What did you learn in Sunday School this morning? And what did you get for your birthday that you liked best of all?" Then I ask them if they have a verse of Scripture they would like to quote for us. Our children are memorizing Scripture verses by the dozens, and they are inspiring their parents to do the same thing. Then the whole church sings "Happy Birthday" to the children. If no one has had a birthday that week, I ask for volunteers to quote verses of Scripture to us.

This is a favorite time for our whole church. Kids do say the craziest things. They make some of the most hilarious statements that you could ever imagine and we all enjoy it.

Children look forward to this time. They often tell me weeks in advance that their birthday is approaching. They stop me in the halls and quote for me the verses they have just memorized. If for some reason I fail to call them to the front, they feel slighted and are quick to remind me that I forgot them. Jesus loved little children, and so do I. I am their friend, and they are mine.

The Church and Little Children

Our church does many things to show its interest in and love for little children. When a baby is born, I visit the parents in the hospital and offer a prayer of thanks to God for the child. We place a red carnation on the Lord's Supper table the next Sunday in honor of the child, and I announce the news of the birth to our congregation.

On the Sunday following Mother's Day, we observe Parents' dedication day. We encourage parents who have had babies born during the past twelve months to bring the children to the sanctuary that morning, and we have a brief time of dedication for the parents.

We continually work at having the finest preschool, day-care, kindergarten, Sunday School, music, missions, and recreation progam possible for little children.

When a child begins to think about accepting Christ and being baptized, I encourage the parents to bring the child to my study for a conference. In this conference, we talk about the importance of this decision and what it means to be a Christian. Then I give them a booklet entitled *Christ, Children, and His Church*. I ask children to work through the book and then come back to see me when they have finished. I tell them that they may ask their parents to help them as they work through the book. This is oftentimes as helpful to the parents as it is to the child. I encourage the parents to be available to assist the child, but only when help is requested. I make it clear that it is the children's responsibility to work through the book and ask for help if they want it.

This booklet serves two purposes. It reenforces what I

have told the child about becoming a Christian and church membership, and it serves as a delaying tactic for those children who are not really ready to make a genuine commitment to Christ. If a child has expressed an interest in joining the church simply because a friend did, he usually loses interest before he completes the book. The child lays it aside and does not mention it again until he is ready.

I had this experience with my own daughter when she was nine years old. One Sunday her best friend accepted Christ and joined the church. The next day she asked me for one of the books. I took it home to her and told her I would help her with it whenever she asked. That night she worked through chapter 1. She then laid the book aside and didn't pick it up again for a full year. By that time, she was ready to make a genuine commitment to Christ and worked through the book to completion in just a few days.

Of course, children may make a profession of faith any time I give an invitation. But I encourage them to visit me first. Parents are greatly concerned that their children understand what they are doing and make a meaningful decision for Christ. I am too. This is an effort to help guarantee that.

Pastor, if you will pay attention to little children, not only will they love you but also their parents will love you and the whole church will love you. Just last week one of our ladies wrote me a letter in which she said:

"DEAR BROTHER PAUL,

". . . there are two things you do in the church services that I hope you'll always continue to do: One, chat with the little children on Sunday night. And, two, meet down the aisle those coming to make commitments. These things reflect such love and warmth that you will never be forgotten for doing them."

11
Putting a Spark in Sunday Night

Sunday night worship is in danger of extinction in many places. There was a time when Sunday evening worship was the most exciting, most popular, and best attended service of the church.

The little country church that I occasionally visited as a boy would have a faithful few present for Sunday morning services, but Sunday night everyone came to church—even the non-Christians of the community. I have often seen men standing outside the church leaning their elbows on the window sill, listening to the sermon through an open window. Many of the men would simply stand outside under the trees and talk, but at least they were there. Going to church on Sunday night in those days was a social event. It was a time to get together with people you did not see during the rest of the week.

But that was before the days of television, fishing lakes, and the wide use of the automobile. That was before people were afraid to get out at night.

Today, in many churches, Sunday evening attendance has dwindled down to almost nothing. If you want your church to grow, you must put a spark in Sunday evening worship. This gathering of the church should become one of the most enjoyable and meaningful services you have. Fortunately, our sanctuary is almost packed every Sunday night. Several things contribute to this.

Build a Great Fellowship

One of the keys to putting a spark in Sunday night worship is to build a great fellowship among your people. What does the word *fellowship* conjure up in your mind when you hear it? For most people it means punch and cookies at an after-church party. The word actually describes the caring and sharing spirit that ought to exist among God's people.

There is a beautiful illustration of this spirit from the life of the apostle Paul. As a prisoner of Rome, he was on his way to the Imperial City for trial. He had never been to Rome before and had never met the Christians who lived there. However, they were well-aware of one another, and he had corresponded with them as his Letter to the Romans indicates.

There must have been tremors in Paul's heart as he approached the threshold of the capital of the world. How would a little tentmaker fare in the greatest city on earth? The Christians in Rome must have anticipated his feelings. So, when they heard that Paul's ship was going to land on the coast of Italy, forty-three miles away, they made the long journey on foot just to meet him and accompany him the rest of the way. Luke gave us a beautiful commentary on the effect it had on Paul. He wrote, "Whom when Paul saw, he thanked God, and took courage" (Acts 28:15). The presence of these Roman Christians strengthened Paul's sagging spirits. He again realized that he was a part of a worldwide fellowship. So, far from his native land, he was at home because these were his brothers.

These early Christians loved one another and were an encouragement to one another even before they met. This is one of the secrets to the growth of Christianity in the first century. We must build this kind of caring and sharing community—especially on Sunday night—if we are to grow in our century also.

Sing Folk Music

Music can do more to put a spark in Sunday evening worship than anything else you can do. So, on Sunday night we sing the triumphant, victorious, and joyous music of our faith. We sing music that is aimed for the heart. We sing folk music.

At a Beverly Hills party given for Britain's Prince Philip in 1966, a Britisher asked jazz artist Louis Armstrong if he were going to change his style to folk music, then much in vogue. "Man," said Louie, "all music's folk music. Nobody but folks listen to or play music. I ain't never heard no horses singing."

Christian music should be folk music—the kind people sing or hum to themselves during the week. Music aimed at the head belongs on the concert stage. Music aimed at the feet belongs at a hoedown. Music aimed at the hips belongs in a night club. But music that aims at the heart belongs in the house of God.

We make use of many groups on Sunday night: Children's choir, Youth choirs, men's choir, Senior Adults' choir, quartets, mixed ensembles, and solos. When our Children's choir and our Youth choirs sing, we can always expect an extra large crowd because their parents come to hear them. Last Sunday night our Senior Adult choir sang, and one of our ladies in her eighties played several hymns on a harmonica. The people responded with a hearty applause at the conclusion of every hymn she played. They thoroughly enjoyed it, and her life was made more meaningful because of it.

Applause in the Church

Applause in the church bothers some people, but not me. Applause is a way of showing approval or agreement with what has been said or sung. We need some way to do that. It is as natural to make some kind of response in church as it is in a theater or a sports event. We are emotional people, and we need to share our feelings. The traditional way to do this in churches is by the use of the word *Amen*. *Amen* is a much misunderstood word today. Most people use it to indicate a full stop to prayer. We use it to mean *the end*. It is like *sincerely yours* at the close of a letter. However, it was originally a great, powerful, strong word of assent. It means "so be it." I like it. I commend it. I wish we would use it more.

One reason Paul did not approve of speaking in tongues in public worship was that no one could understand what was being said and thus could not affirm the truth by saying "Amen" (1 Cor. 14:16). Obviously, the church service was not to be just one man preaching and everyone else listening. It was to be the pastor preaching and the people affirming what was being said.

I can see why people prefer applause to saying amen. Applause lends itself to a group response while the saying of amen is one individual's reponse. If I say amen, I do it alone unless the leader prompts us by saying, "And all the people said . . ." That kind of response is not spontaneous. When I say amen, I do it alone for I am through before you can join me. However, if someone begins to applaud and I share the feeling, I can join in without calling attention to myself. It becomes a spontaneous group response.

I don't even object to occasionally clapping hands in rhythm to music in the church. The Bible speaks of it often in connection with worship (Ps. 47:1). So there is certainly nothing irreverent about it.

Most of us feel uncomfortable with this because it is not a part of our tradition. We didn't grow up on it, and it smacks of shallow emotionalism.

One thing is sure. When a congregation is alive, happy, and vibrant, it will respond. Applause is much to be preferred over the dull, dead, formal, lifeless services of most traditional churches today. So, while I do not commend applause after everything that happens in the church, I think it is good when it is spontaneous expression of the heart.

Observing the Ordinances

Never was there a man who cared less about ritual and ceremony than Jesus. There was little place for these things in his personal and intimate relationship with the Heavenly Father. The only two ceremonies that Jesus inaugurated and taught us to perpetuate were baptism and the Lord's Supper. Both of them center in the gospel and our redemption in Christ.

The Lord's Supper symbolizes what happened to Jesus when he went to the cross. Baptism symbolizes what happened to us when we went to the cross. When Jesus went to the cross his body was broken and his blood was shed. When we went to the cross, the old person, dead in sin, was resurrected to a newness of life. So in a real sense the Lord's Supper is a way of declaring what we believe about Christ, and baptism is the way of declaring what we have experienced in Christ.

You can put a spark in Sunday night by magnifying these two ordinances of our Lord.

Baptism

We baptize every Sunday night. I begin the service by explaining from the baptistry the meaning of baptism. There are many visitors from other denominations in our church on Sunday night, and this gives me an opportunity to explain what the Bible teaches and what we believe about baptism.

I point out that baptism is for believers only. There is no record in the New Testament of anyone ever being baptized who was not first a believer in Christ.

Secondly, I point out that baptism is to be by immersion. That's what the word *baptize* meant in Jesus' day. The word *baptize* was often used to describe the dyeing of a garment by putting it completely under.

Finally, I point out that baptism is only a symbol. There is no magic in the water. Baptism is not a means of salvation. It does not wash away any sins. The water we baptize in is the same kind of water we drink and the same kind of water we take a bath in. The significance is in what it symbolizes. It symbolizes death, burial, and resurrection. The water represents the grave. Lowering a person into the water symbolizes death and burial. Raising the person up symbolizes resurrection (Rom. 6:3-5).

Baptism is a way of declaring two things: what we believe about Jesus and what we have experienced in our own lives. It declares our faith. We believe that Jesus died, was buried, and was raised again on the third day. It declares our experience. We were once dead in trespasses and in sins. But through faith in Christ, we were given new life. We have been resurrected spiritually, so when we are baptized we are saying to all who watch, "This is what I believe about Jesus and this is what I've experienced in my own life."

As I baptize each candidate I ask them to repeat this vow after me:

> I take God as my Father,
> Jesus as my Savior,
> The Holy Spirit as my guide.
> This I do freely,
> Completely,
> And forever.

As I lift the candidate out of the water, the congregation says amen in unison. The vow allows the candidate to make a public commitment to Christ, and it allows the congregation to affirm and approve of what has happened by their amen.

The Lord's Supper

We observe the Lord's Supper once a month. A couple of years ago I came to the conviction that once a quarter was not often enough. Once a week was too often. Once a month seems to be ideal. On the nights that we observe the Lord's Supper, we do not have a sermon. Instead I ask two of our people to share their personal testimonies of what God is doing in their lives.

Nothing is more powerful than one person sharing with another what God is doing in his life. The average church member listens to the lay person with receptive ears. They have a tendency to look upon a preacher as a paid sales representative and to look upon the lay person as a satisfied customer. While the lay person's testimony may not be eloquent or polished, it will have a ring of sincerity about it that makes it believable. We must remember that it is not the height of one's eloquence but the depth of one's sincerity that makes him effective.

Occasionally, on a night when we are observing the

Lord's Supper, I will ask the children to come to the front early in the service. Then I explain the meaning of the Lord's Supper to them. I will pass the plate of bread and an empty cup among them so they can examine them. There are several values in this. For one thing, the children can understand the meaning of the Lord's Supper better.

Second, it keeps those children who have not yet received Christ from feeling completely left out of the service. And it is a teaching opportunity.

As we observe the Lord's Supper, I try to emphasize these basic truths:

(1) It is a time of commemoration. We do this "in remembrance" of the death of our Savior. It is not a means of salvation.

(2) It is a time of examination. The person who partakes of the supper is to "examine himself." We must see beyond the physical elements to understand the spiritual reality that is being symbolized.

(3) It is a time of proclamation. As we observe it, we "show" (proclaim) the Lord's death until he comes again. We are declaring our faith and our commitment to all who are present in that service.

These Lord's Supper services have been some of the most moving and spiritual services I have ever been in. We seldom observe the Lord's Supper without numerous re-dedications and public decisions for Christ.

Biblical Preaching

Of course preaching is always a part of any vital worship service. On Sunday night, my sermons are more expository in nature. I preach many sermon series on Sunday night. Series on "The Life Beyond," "The Twenty-Third Psalm,"

"The Lord's Prayer," "The Sermon on the Mount," and series from books of the Bible are very popular.

Other Things

There are many other things that can enrich Sunday night worship. Sometimes we move our services outside. When I was in San Marcos, we moved our Sunday evening services to the city park every Sunday night in August. The people brought blankets and folding chairs to sit on, and I preached to them in the open air. We even baptized converts in the San Marcos River. We usually followed these outside services with an all-church ice cream or watermelon party. We attracted visitors, won people to Christ, and enriched our Sunday evening worship this way.

In Tyler, we moved into the amphitheater of the city park during the month of August for several years. Now, twice a year we have an all-church picnic at our own lake property. We begin with games and contests in the afternoon, dinner on the grounds, baptizing in the lake, and then worship under the tabernacle. Seven or eight hundred people attend these services.

Sunday night is a vital time to a growing church. Put a spark in the service, and it will help your own church grow.

12
Building a Staff Team

John Wooden, the basketball coach I quoted earlier, once said, "No team with the nation's leading scorer on it has ever won the NCAA Championship." Basketball, as you know, is a team sport. If a team's success depends too much on one player, the team is easier to defeat. All an opponent needs to do is to double-team the star. Stop him and you cripple the whole team. Basketball teams do best and go the farthest when the scoring is balanced and every player makes a vital contribution to the team.

It is the same with a church. As a church grows, the pastor must gather around him a team of workers who share his dreams, his philosophy, and his convictions and who will cooperate with him in doing God's work. After all, one person can do only so much. If a pastor is to multiply his efforts, he must multiply his staff. If staff members feel like a team, act like a team, and work as a team, the church will prosper and grow.

The Team Concept

The team concept for Christian workers is scriptural. The apostle Paul spoke of one who labored with him in the gospel as "true yoke-fellow" (Phil. 4:3). The Greek word Paul used here describes a group of athletes who cooperate as a team. They work in harmony toward a common goal.

Paul used the team concept again when he said, "Stand fast in one spirit, with one mind, striving together for the faith of the gospel" (Phil. 1:27). The word *strive* is also an athletic term. Our mission is to spread the gospel. Like athletes, we are to strain every fiber of our being to get the job done. As we work toward this goal, we are to be of "one spirit," "one mind," and "together." One spirit means unity of feeling. One mind means unity of thought. Together means unity of action. Like a team, with unity of feeling, unity of thought, and unity of action, we are to strive to spread the gospel to all people everywhere.

Since I'm a Texan, the Dallas Cowboys serve as a good illustration of what I'm talking about. A football team has many players. Each man is a professional. Each man has his own position to play. Each man has certain abilities that qualify him for his particular position. And each man has a special assignment. But when the ball is snapped, all eleven men move as a unit—as one man. When each man takes his assignment and does his part, the whole team marches down the field toward the goal.

Between each play, the team huddles to get its signals straight. This is necessary for unity. In the huddle, the quarterback calls the play the team is going to run and then gives them the count on which the ball is to be snapped. The play gives each man his specific assignment and the count enables the team to move as a unit.

While the quarterback calls the play, it does not mean that other team members have no input. They do. The wide receiver may say, "I can beat my man down the sideline." The quarterback may not have seen that and so this information helps him to call a better game. But he is the one who must finally say, "OK, this is the play we are going to run, and this is the count for the snap of the ball. Let's go! Let's score!" Then with one spirit and one mind, they move together as one man toward the goal.

Developing a Good Game Plan

Teamwork requires coordination. We coordinate the work of our staff with two retreats each year and a staff meeting each week.

The two retreats are the times when we develop our game plan. The weekly staff meetings are like a huddle between each play. In the first of our retreats each year, I begin by restating the purpose of our church and challenging our staff about the future. I don't assume that just because they are church workers they have a clear understanding of what our objective is. Our mission is the Great Commission. I keep that before them continuously. Each program we promote and every activity we sponsor is in some way to fit in with this overall objective. If it does not, there is no place for it on our calendar.

Then we do some brainstorming. I ask each staff member to share with us his personal goals in life. I want to know what each man would like to be doing and where he would like to be five years from now. I want to know this so I can help them achieve their own personal goals. When a person is moving toward some meaningful goal of his own, he will be happier and more productive.

Then I ask, "If you had unlimited funds and ample personnel, what would you like to accomplish in your area of work?" This question stretches our imagination and occasionally leads to some good ideas. While we don't have either of these—unlimited funds or ample personnel—it doesn't cost a cent to dream. And sometimes it pays great dividends.

I then ask each staffer to share the plans and programs

he has developed for his area of ministry for the next year. This kind of report requires that hek give careful thought and planning to his entire program in advance. The program is then discussed and evaluated by every member of the staff. Sometimes a staff member has planned too much in his area. Sometimes he has planned too little.

No one is exempt from criticism and evaluation, including me. Everyone freely expresses his opinion about every other person's area of work. After all, we are a team. We are moving toward the same goal, and we want to complement one another. I'm not interested in having my own way, but in finding the best way. So, I try to keep an open mind to new ideas and new ways. I need and welcome the evaluation of my staff.

In the second retreat, we plan our church calendar. We take those plans and programs that have been agreed upon and put them all together in one unified calendar. This necessitates changing some plans and altering some programs to avoid conflicts. All programs have to fit together in a unified way.

The Weekly Huddle

Our weekly staff meeting takes place each Monday. We begin with a lunch prepared by our church hostess and served in the Family Life Center. This is a time of informal and enjoyable fellowship. After lunch, Dennis Parrott, our administrator and minister of education, distributes a written report of the stewardship, additions, Sunday School attendance, and staff visits from the previous week. Then he reviews the calendar for the week and discusses any programs, plans, or problems that he knows about.

Our associate pastor, John LaNoue, then makes weekly staff assignments. Since every member of our staff is a minister, I feel they should minister. Every staff member is assigned visitation prospects and is expected to report the number of visits made on a report form at the next staff meeting. Every member of our staff visits the hospital on a rotating basis. I want our staff to know and to mix with our people. I want our people to know and to appreciate every member of our staff. We all, therefore, benefit from contacts made in the hospital. Also, assignments are made for the reading of the Scriptures and leading in prayer at each of our morning worship services. I want everyone on our staff to be before our people in public worship and to share in leading it.

Then each staff member shares any program, plans, or problems he would like to discuss. I close our staff meeting with thirty minutes of staff improvement time. We discuss subjects like how to be a better witness, how to motivate people, how to better manage time, and how to plan better. I don't assume that just because a person is on a church staff that he knows all of these things. I don't assume that he will work hard. And I don't even assume that he is a self-starter. I feel that it is my responsibility to help all of my staff develop into the best servants of our Lord and his church they can possibly be. This necessitates continual training and motivation.

Following our staff meeting, we spend the afternoon in recreation together in our Family Life Center. Some of us play racquetball, others bowl, and others participate in other activities. Our staff members like one another, respect one another, and enjoy being with one another for lunch and for recreation.

What I Expect!

Teamwork involves responsibilities—each person doing his job well. We, therefore, reasonably expect certain things of one another. I expect a lot out of myself, and I expect a lot out of my staff.

What do I expect from my staff members? I expect dedication to Christ. We are to love him, have a personal devotional life, practice personal holiness, witness, and tithe. A worldly staff cannot build a spiritual church. The people will seldom rise above their leadership.

I expect loyalty. We are to love one another, pray for one another, and support one another. We are all to speak well of one another and protect and defend one another at all times. There is no place for jealousy, backbiting, and criticism on our staff. If we don't like what another person is doing, we are to say so to him, not to members of the church.

I expect professionalism. Every member of our staff is an expert in his field. He needs to know more about his area of work than any one else does. In fact, if my staff does not know more about their area of work than I do, we are in trouble. We are to be as good at our job as any other professional person in our church is at his work.

I expect growth. We should all be moving toward excellence. We are to continue to study, read, attend conferences, and grow to our fullest potential. Stagnation is intolerable. Our mission, message, and Master are always the same. But we must be creative and fresh in our methods. We must stay out of ruts.

I expect leadership. Each staff member is a leader and is expected to exercise that gift. Committees do not lead. They only confirm and evaluate leadership. Every staff person is to dream, set goals, develop plans, present definite proposals, anticipate difficulties, and communicate effectively. They are to enlist, train, motivate, and supervise people to get the job done. We are to plan our work and work our plan. We expect execution, not excuses.

I expect hard work. No one can be a success working eight hours a day. Long days and sleepless nights are the price of excellence in any endeavor. I expect my staff to be at work on time and to be diligent with their time. They are not to spend their days in extraneous activities. They are to be as diligent in their work as if they worked at any other job. Staff members should gear up or get out. Laziness by a Christian worker is unacceptable.

I expect discipline. This involves making assigned visits, turning in reports, following the church calendar, setting the right priorities, being a good time manager, following administrative structure, abiding by church policy, and living within the budget. It also involves keeping in good physical shape so we can be at our very best in God's service.

I expect a good attitude. A person's attitude more than his aptitude determines his altitude in life. A humble, teachable spirit is a necessity. A know-it-all-attitude and an argumentative spirit creates strife, and a bad temper spells trouble.

When we are wrong we should be quick to admit it and to ask for forgiveness if necessary. It doesn't hurt any of us to "eat crow" once in a while. In twenty-five years of pastoring, I have eaten crow every way it can be cooked—boiled, baked, barbecued, and even "extra crispy." I don't like it any way or any time, but I can assure you that while it is hard to swallow it won't kill you.

I expect good communication. We must keep each other informed about all plans and programs and we must share our honest feelings.

I expect congeniality. We must love and get along with others. There is no excuse for abrasiveness. We must use tact in all of our dealings. Tact is the ability to build a fire under a person without making him boil. We should never use a sledgehammer when a tack hammer will do. We are to motivate, not alienate, people.

I expect submission to authority. I do not think of the other staff members as working for me. They work with me. I respect them and give them much freedom. However, there are times when I must say no to their desires. When that is necessary I expect them to accept it gracefully.

After Billy Martin was fired by the owner of the New York Yankees for insubordination, a reporter saw on the wall of Billy's vacated office this motto:

"Rule 1: the boss is always right!

Rule 2: when the boss is wrong, remember rule number 1."

Like it or not, it can be no other way. Somebody has to have the final say.

The greatest human asset a church can have is a good staff. They should be paid well and treated with respect. The laborer is worthy of both (1 Tim. 5:17-18; Heb. 13:7). I believe that I have the greatest staff in the whole world. They are capable, dedicated, sincere, loyal, and hardworking. I do everything I can to encourage them and show my appreciation for them. I brag on them in staff meetings, from the pulpit, in our church paper, and I write them letters occasionally. I try to keep in mind that people do not live by bread alone. They need buttering once in a while.

On Tuesday of each week, I take one of my staff members to lunch. This is just a time for fellowship. As our church grows larger and our staff members have less and less personal contact, this is imperative if we are to get to know one another.

I love my staff and I want our people to love them and

follow them also. The best thing that can happen to me is for every one of them to be a success. The better they do, the better I look.

So, if you want to build a growing church, build a good staff. Set a good example before them. Be reasonable and fair in your expectations of them, and treat them like brothers. If you'll do that, your church will grow.

13
Financing by Faith

A lady listened patiently as her friend complained about how expensive it was to raise her little boy. When she was through, the lady replied, "Perhaps you didn't know it, but I had a little boy like yours once. He was forever costing me money. He was always outgrowing his clothes, wearing out his shoes, and tearing his shirts. It was just one expense after another. Then, when he was eleven years old, he died. And, do you know what? Since he died, he hasn't cost me a cent."

Growing churches, like growing boys, cost money. If a church is sterile and arthritic, it doesn't cost much to keep it going. But if it is growing, alive, and vibrant, it will be expensive. It will require new buildings, better programs, extra literature, more promotion, and a larger staff. All of this costs money.

While we expect this and are thankful for it, it does pose a problem. Where do we get the money? How do we finance the church?

When All Else Fails

Horace Greeley once received a letter from a woman stating that her church was in distressing financial straits. The congregation had tried oyster suppers, grab bags, box socials, everything. "Would Mr. Greeley be so kind as to suggest some new advice to keep a struggling church from disbanding?"

The editor replied, "Try religion."

That's the philosophy that I subscribe to. The best way to raise money for a church is for that church to be what a church should be and do the work of the Lord. The best stewardship promotion is not to have a month-long campaign with pledge cards, subtle pressure, and an every-member canvass. It is to give people a program that is worthy of their support.

Roger Babson, devout Christian, churchman, and financial expert, said something similar to this when he wrote, "One reason why most churches have so much difficulty in raising money for any purpose is because the people to whom they go for money have received so little concrete benefits from the institution."

If week by week God's word is preached and the people are blessed, if they like their church, and if it meets their needs, they will come. If they come, they will give. If they don't come and if their needs are not being met, you can appeal to them all you want to and they will never give but a token amount. They will just get mad and complain, "All the church wants is money."

So build an exciting, loving, ministering fellowship and the people will support it gladly. All you'll need to do is to teach them what God's Word says, inform them of the need, and they will respond.

Turning Watermelons into Missions

When people are happy and thankful, they will want to give. One Sunday morning in the spring of 1975 I announced to our church that we needed one hundred dollars a month for the next year in order to put a full-time pastor on the field of the mission church we were sponsoring in Mexico. That night one of our deacons said to me, "Pastor, when I was seventeen years old I left home and went to California. I had no money, no job, and for several days I had nothing to eat. Then one day I saw a young Mexican boy with a wagon load of watermelons. I asked him if he would give me one to eat. He did. I was so hungry that I almost ate the rind. Since that time, I have been looking for a way to repay that Mexican boy. If you'll let me, I want to give that hundred dollars a month to put the mission pastor on the field."

That's what gratitude will do for people. It makes them want to give. It turns watermelons into missions.

Try Faith Financing

For years, we have practiced faith financing in our church. Here is how it works. First, we plan what we believe to be an adequate church budget. Next, we present it to the people for their approval. Then we trust God and trust our people to meet those needs. I realize that many will disagree with me. We sign no pledge cards. We raise no hands. We have no public demonstration. We only ask for a personal, heartfelt commitment between our people and the Lord concerning their stewardship.

I have no argument with those who want to sign stewardship commitment cards, but it is not my way. Can't we trust God for anything? Can't we trust our people? Must we have everything in writing? Where is our faith?

I do see some value in pledge cards. They help a church know how much money it can expect to receive during the year. However, I know of no church that revises its budget downward when the people fail to subscribe it. They continue with their adopted budget whether it is pledged or not. To me, that seems to nullify the purpose of pledging. Second, signing a card does help bring people to a point of

decision. Many people procrastinate. They have good intentions but never act on them. To sign a pledge card does
require that a person come to some definite decision.

We do sign pledge cards on building programs. The
reason for this is that the lending institutions consider
pledges a valid indication of people's intentions. But apart
from the fact that they want it, I find them unnecessary
even in building programs.

Our emphasis consists of three things: information, inspiration, and dedication. We inform our people of our
needs and what our church is doing for the cause of Christ.
Then we have personal testimonies and a sermon or two to
teach and to inspire them.

Dedication is the final step in our emphasis. We close
our campaign with Tithers' Demonstration Day and Commitment Day. On that day, I ask everyone in our congregation to bring at least a tithe of their income that we may
demonstrate to ourselves the tremendous giving potential
of our church. If they have never tithed before, I ask them
to do it that one day. If they never intend to tithe again, I
ask them to still do it at least that once. I preach that Sunday
morning on Christian stewardship and call on our people to
make a personal commitment to the Lord concerning their
stewardship for the next year.

It Works for Us

Faith financing helps us to keep money in the right perspective. Some churches spend more time and energy on
pledging their budget than on any other single thing they
do. And the only time they call on their members is when
they want them to make a pledge to the church. I refuse to
do that.

For us, faith financing has worked. It is a simple but

sufficient strategy for stewardship. This year our peoples' gifts exceeded our $1,386,300 budget by over $94,000. Faith financing seems to please God and our people. It takes a lot of pressure off the staff, our people enjoy it, and it puts stewardship in the right perspective.

Seven Principles of Stewardship

In our stewardship emphasis, we attempt to focus on the soul and not on the pocketbook. We focus on what the Lord wants rather than upon the church needs.

This is the emphasis the apostle Paul made to the church at Philippi. They had sent him a sacrificial gift while he was in prison at Rome. Paul thanked them for their gift but made it quite clear that his gratitude was not because he needed the gift, rather because he desired fruit from their lives (Phil. 4:17). In short, Paul said that they needed to give the gift far more then he needed to receive it. And while they had given sacrificially, their gift being compared to a wonderful sacrifice laid upon the altar to God, they would not be impoverished. Paul said, "But my God shall supply all your need according to his riches in glory by Christ Jesus" (Phil. 4:19).

With this in mind, there are seven stewardship principles we emphasize.

1. Everything belongs to God—"The earth is the Lord's and the fulness thereof; the world, and they that dwell therein" (Ps. 24:1).
2. God has entrusted his world and everything in it to us. We are stewards of God's creation. He expects us to use and to manage wisely all that belongs to him.
3. God blesses those who honor him with their possessions (Prov. 3:9-10). No gift leaves anyone poorer. We enrich ourselves when we give. Our

withholding does not impoverish God at all. It only impoverishes us. When we rob God of that which is rightfully his, we court economic disaster (Mal. 3:8-12).

4. The tithe is the basic expression of stewardship. The word *tithe* means "one-tenth." The giving of the tithe is always a recognition of God's ownership of everything. It symbolizes the whole.

5. Giving beyond the tithe is grace. We are not under the law but we are under grace. Grace in our hearts does not cause us to do less than the law demands but more. We need to move away from set amounts and to call for growth in grace, rather than just giving 10 percent. I'm convinced that the true beginning of Christian stewardship is a clean break with the false god mammon and a complete self-surrender to the love of God in Christ.

6. A systematic approach to giving is proper. Paul said, "Upon the first day of the week let every one of you lay by him in store, as God hath prospered him, that there be no gatherings when I come" (1 Cor. 16:2).

7. Giving money can never be a substitute for giving yourself. Stewardship must never be a gimmick to get money. It is a deeply religious act of concentration. It is the way to get people. You learn to love what you work for and give to. Where your treasure is there will your heart be also. Giving strengthens your faith, deepens your joy, and broadens your witness.

If people first give themselves to the Lord, they will never have any trouble with the tithe.

How Can We Do It?

I've often heard people say, "When we first promised to tithe, we didn't see how we could do it." That is one of the secrets. The person who can see how he can do it expresses no faith. And without faith it is impossible to please God. If you can trust God for your eternal salvation, surely you can trust him for your daily needs. If you can trust God to take care of you spiritually, surely you can trust him to take care of you materially. Giving is not a matter of financial resources, it is a matter of love, faith, and commitment.

Churches need faith just like individuals do. It is high time that we start putting faith into our stewardship. Give the people a good church program. Teach them what God says about stewardship. Make them aware of the needs of the church. Then trust them and trust God to meet your needs. This is a simple and sufficient program of Christian stewardship for a growing church.

Appendix 1
Where We Stand

Introduction

Archimedes, the famous Greek mathematician and physicist, said that if he were given three things he could move the earth off its axis. "Give me a standing place out yonder in space, a fulcrum, and a lever long enough and strong enough, and I will move the world!"

A place to stand—that's what we need. In fact, we must have it if we are going to be a moving force in the world. Peter Marshall, the great Presbyterian preacher, once prayed, "God help us to stand for something lest we fall for anything." Those who stand for nothing lack the strength and stability to withstand error and thus can never be world-movers for God.

Where do we stand? What do we believe? What is our position on the great issues of the Bible? To some people Baptists are known more by what they are against than by what they are for. We have always stood against social evils. Gladly, we are advocates of social righteousness. We make no apologies for that. However, the things we are for are far more important than those we are against.

This booklet was written to express in positive terms what we stand for. It is an individual effort to state clearly and concisely where our church stands doctrinally. This is in no sense a binding statement of faith and message. We

Baptists have no creed. We have always shied away from anything that resembles a creed or statement of belief to which people are forced to subscribe.

Baptists have often been accused of being narrow-minded and bigoted. The opposite is true. Baptists have always stood for religious liberty for all people. We are among the most broad-minded of all people in religion. We grant to all people the right to believe and worship or not to believe and not to worship. However, there are some great truths we all hold in common. This is an effort to state some of those common denominators. It is offered with the prayer that you too might come to the same settled and fixed conviction and join us as we help move the world for God.

December 22, 1975

I. We Stand on the Lordship of Jesus Christ

We believe that Jesus Christ is the eternal Son of God and both the Savior and Lord of all who believe and trust in him (Acts 2:36).

The facts of his life are simple. He was foretold by the prophets (Isa. 7:14); born of a virgin (Matt. 1:18-23); lived a life of perfect obedience to God (Heb. 4:15). He preached with authority (Matt. 8:28-29); performed miracles (Acts 2:22); died to pay for our sins (1 Peter 3:18); was raised from the dead (1 Cor. 15:4); appeared to people again (1 Cor. 15:5-9). He ascended to heaven to be the mediator (peacemaker) between God and us (1 Tim. 2:5-6). One day he will return to the earth to judge it (Rom. 14:10-12). Until then he dwells in the hearts of all believers as the living and ever-present Lord. His death on the cross was a payment for our sins and the means by which we are forgiven and brought into a right relationship with God (saved) (Rom. 3:25-26).

By virtue of his life, death, and resurrection, he is the master or ruler of life (Phil. 2:5-11). And the right to rule our lives now belongs to him (Matt. 28:18). People have no right to sit in judgment upon his teachings or to choose what teachings they will obey. To Christ is due complete obedience.

To be a Christian is not just to accept a philosophy of life, nor to seek to live up to a code of ethics, nor to observe certain ceremonies. To be a Christian is to have a personal relationship with the Lord of life. He is the object of faith and devotion. It is he whom we worship, trust, serve, and obey.

Jesus is both Savior and Lord (Acts 2:36). We stand on that!

II. We Stand on the Free Gift of Salvation

We believe that salvation is the free gift of God that comes through faith in Jesus Christ and cannot be earned. Salvation means the redemption, or recovery, of the whole person from the power and consequences of sin, bringing that person into a right relationship with God. For the past it means forgiveness from the guilt of sin. For the present it means deliverance from the control of sin. For the future it means deliverance from the punishment of sin. This salvation is called eternal life. It is a life that begins the moment we believe in Jesus and continues into eternity.

We are saved by faith in Jesus who died as the substitute for our sins (Heb. 9:12). We are not saved by being good (moral, honest, kind), nor by being religious (by being baptized, going to church, giving money). These things are but the outgrowth of salvation, not the means. We are saved by grace (unmerited, unearned favor) through faith (reliance on) and not by our own good works (Eph. 2:8-9).

There are at least three kinds of faith. One kind is intellectual faith, which is believing facts with the mind, such as believing in George Washington or any other historical person. A second kind of faith is temporary faith, which is believing with your emotions, such as in a time of crisis or emergency. At such times, almost everyone believes enough to pray. However, the prayers and trust cease when the crisis passes. The third kind is saving faith, which is trusting in Jesus and Jesus alone to make you right with God. It is commitment to him as the only hope of forgiveness.

There is just one way to salvation and that is Jesus. Some people think there are many ways to become right with God and to go to heaven. Not so! Jesus is the only way to salvation (Acts 4:12). No one can be right with God except through faith in him (John 14:6).

There is just one way to Jesus and that is through faith. There are not *many* roads to Christ. It is through faith (commitment) alone that we come to him. Without faith we cannot come to God (Heb. 11:6).

However, there are many ways to faith. We can come to faith in nearly any church (denomination) or in no church. The important thing is not the church attended but the faith possessed. We recognize as fellow Christians all people who follow Christ, regardless of their denominational alignment.

The simple conditions of salvation revealed in the New Testament are as follows: (1) conviction of sin (John 16:8); (2) repentance from sin, a change of attitude that leads to a change in action (Acts 3:19; Matt. 19:28-31); (3) faith in Jesus Christ; and (4) confession of that faith (Rom. 10:9-10).

Salvation is the free gift of God to all who commit themselves to Jesus Christ as Lord and Savior. We stand on that!

III. We Stand on the Authority of the Scriptures

We believe that the Scriptures, embracing both the Old and the New Testaments, are the inspired Word of God and are the sole authority for our faith and practice. They have God as their Author, salvation as their end, and truth for their matter. They reveal God's idea of what is right and the principles by which God shall judge us and, therefore, they will remain until the end of the world.

The Bible is inspired, which means that God revealed himself and his message to his messengers (Heb. 1:1), that the Holy Spirit enlightened their minds so they could grasp or comprehend the revealed truth (1 John 16:13-15), and then God moved upon these men like a mighty wind to guide them to deliver or record that message for all ages (2 Pet. 1:20-21). The evidences of inspiration are many—the Bible's own claims, fulfilled prophecy, its amazing unity, its endurance of criticism and persecution and the truthfulness of its message. It contains truth found nowhere else and truth that could not be discovered by human reasoning. Since its teaching is given by God, it is fully reliable and adequate for all of our spiritual needs.

The Bible is authoritative, which means it is our rule and guide for faith and practice. No person, board, council or other writing can supersede its importance to us.

The Bible is eternal, which means that its message is never out-of-date. Other books come and go, but the truth of the Bible is timeless. It was true yesterday. It is true today. It shall be true tomorrow, and if the earth shall last a thousand years, it shall still be true (1 Pet. 1:23-25).

The Bible is sufficient, which means it contains all the religious truth that we need. Other books may be helpful, but none other is necessary. It is completely adequate to teach us what to believe and how to live (2 Tim. 3:16-17).

The main theme of the Bible is redemption (bringing people into a right relationship with God). Its primary purpose is to introduce lost people (those alienated from God because of their sins) to Christ and then to lead them on to spiritual maturity in their daily lives. It makes no claims to being a book of science, history, philosophy, or psychology, yet it contains true elements of all of these, and more. It was given to show us how to become right with God. This is evidenced by the fact that only two brief chapters deal with the creation of all the universe and fully one-third of each of the four Gospels deals with the last week of Jesus' life. The cross and the events surrounding it are described in vivid detail. The great purpose of the Gospels and all the Scriptures is obviously to tell us that Christ died to bring us into a right relationship with God. Through a study of the Scriptures, we learn the way to salvation (2 Tim. 3:15).

The Bible is the inspired, authoritative, eternal, sufficient, and reliable word of God. We stand on that!

IV. We Stand on the Immersion of Believers

We believe three key truths about baptism:

1. Baptism is a symbolic act of confession and identification. It has no power in itself to take away our sin and make us right with God. Just as a wedding ring is an identifying symbol of our marriage commitment, so baptism is an identifying symbol of our Christian commitment. What does

baptism symbolize? It symbolizes death, burial, and resurrection (Rom. 6:3-4). The water represents a grave. Lowering a person into the water symbolizes burial. Raising that person from the water symbolizes resurrection. When a person is baptized, he is saying "I believe in Christ who died, was buried, and arose again." At the same time, it symbolizes the believer's death to sin, burial of the old life, and the resurrection to a new life. It also points forward to the future resurrection of the dead. When people have come to faith in Christ, they should then be baptized (Acts 2:41-42; 8:35-39).

The idea that baptism helped make people right with God did not appear in Christian teachings until late in the second and early in the third centuries. In the first century, false teachers sought to change God's plan of salvation. They changed it from unearned favor through faith to salvation by religious ceremonies (Acts 15; Gal. 2; Col. 2:16-23). But all these were rejected by the early Christians.

However, by the late second and early third centuries, salvation by baptism came to be accepted by the group which later evolved into the Roman Catholic Church. Today the idea of salvation by baptism persists in Catholicism and to a degree in many other churches.

The Lord's Supper is the other church ordinance (Matt. 26:26-29; Mark 14:22-25; Luke 22:17-20; 1 Cor. 11:23-26). Baptists believe that it also is symbolical. The elements merely symbolize the body and blood of Jesus. There is no saving power in taking them.

Like the meaning in baptism, the elements portray what Jesus did for our salvation. Both are visual aids whereby believers portray the basis and experience of their saving relationship with Jesus Christ.

Jesus did not say when or how often believers should observe the Lord's Supper. He instituted it on Thursday night. New Testament Christians observed it on the Lord's Day. But Jesus did say that as often as we take the Lord's Supper we proclaim to the world how he died until he comes again (1 Cor. 11:26). Both the bread and the cup are to be taken to remember his death (1 Cor. 11:24-25). So both baptism and the Lord's Supper look back to what Jesus has done to make us right with God and forward to his second coming.

Both of these are sermons in symbol of Jesus' redeeming work and promised return. Baptism is an initiatory ordinance to be administered to the believer only one time. The Lord's Supper is a continuing ordinance to be observed at stated intervals throughout the believer's life until Jesus comes again.

2. We believe that baptism is for believers only. It is reserved for those who have first trusted Christ as their Savior. There is no record in the Bible of anyone except a believer being baptized. In the scores of times it tells us about people being baptized, it always emphasizes that they first believed in Christ. For this reason we do not baptize babies. Babies do not believe, nor do they need to. They have no awareness of God and no guilt of sin. They inherit a nature and environment inclined towards rebellion and disobedience against God, and as soon as they are capable of moral action, they become sinners by choice and are under condemnation. When that time comes, the child needs to trust Christ personally for salvation and then to be baptized in confession of that faith. Some denominations that baptize babies believe that babies are born guilty of sin because of what Adam (the first man) did. The child inherits his guilt. And they believe that baptism washes away that

original sin. They believe that if the baby died without baptism it would be forever separated from God. The Bible doesn't teach that. Babies aren't born guilty of sin and baptism does not wash away sin. Babies are safe and secure with a loving God until they knowingly rebel against him. When that time comes, they become rebellious and disobedient by choice and need to accept Christ as the One who can make them right with God. They are then ready to be baptized as a confession of their faith.

Others explain their baptism of babies as just a dedication service. If that's all it is, why does the pastor usually say "I baptize you" as he sprinkles the child? If it is a parental dedication, then why not say "I dedicate you" or better still, why do anything to the child at all? After all, no one can dedicate someone else to anything. We can dedicate our money and our homes because they have no choice; but people are always free to make their own decisions. They cannot be dedicated by anyone else in the fullest sense of the word.

3. We believe baptism is to be by immersion. The word *immerse* means to put under water. Some denominations sprinkle instead of immerse. There is little doubt that the word *baptize* meant "immerse" in Jesus' day and that this was the form of baptism used in the early New Testament church.

William Barclay, Presbyterian author of *The Daily Bible Commentary,* says about baptism in the Bible " . . . for baptism was by total immersion" (The letters to Timothy, Titus and Philemon, p. 99).

Laurence Christenson, author and minister of the Trinity Lutheran Church in San Pedro, California, since 1960, said of John the Baptist, "He could baptize each one only as they would stop 'doing' and allow him to immerse them."

The Interpreter's Bible, a Methodist commentary, says that immersion was "almost certainly the customary form of baptism in the primitive church" (Comm. on Romans, p. 474).

The baptistry, part of the duomo (cathedral) in Florence, Italy, dates back to the eleventh century. Many famous Florentines were baptized there, including Dante. A large mural in this building depicts John immersing Jesus in the Jordan. Many other cathedrals in Europe have murals or mosaics showing Jesus' baptism. All show him being immersed. The Roman Catholics admit that they simply changed the method.

Since Jesus meant immersion when he taught us to go and baptize, we feel we have no right to change and practice it in any other way.

Why do we baptize those who join our church from other denominations? It most certainly is not because we doubt that they are Christians. Baptism has nothing to do with that.

New Testament baptism requires three things to be valid. Candidates must adhere to, trust in, and rely on Christ to make them right with God. It must be symbolical in its meaning. And it must be by immersion. If one of these ingredients is missing, the act is not complete.

When Paul came to Ephesus, he found some disciples who had no knowledge of the Holy Spirit. Realizing they had a deficiency in their Christian experience, he asked them what beliefs they had acknowledged at their baptism. They replied that they had believed what John the Baptist had taught. Paul then pointed out that John's baptism was to demonstrate a desire to turn from rebellion to obedience to God and that those receiving his baptism must then go on to believe in Jesus. When they heard this, they were baptized in the name of the Lord Jesus (Acts 19:1-5).

The point of the passage is this: Although the form of their baptism was correct (immersion) and the meaning was close (a symbol), their experience was inadequate (they had no saving knowledge of Christ), so their baptism was not valid. It takes the right kind of person (a believer) being baptized in the right way (immersion) for the right reason (a symbol) to be authentic Christian baptism.

Jesus commanded us to go into all the world and make disciples, immersing them in the name of the Father, the Son, and the Holy Spirit (Matt. 28:19-20). We stand on that!

V. We Stand on the Fellowship of the Church

We believe that the church is a local fellowship of Christians who in mutual love for one another meet for the common purpose of worship, service, and encouragement.

1. *The church is divine in its origin.* It is not just another fraternal order or a service club. It was founded by Christ himself (Matt. 16:18) and belongs to God (1 Tim. 3:15). Christ is its head and leader (Eph. 5:23). That's why our church is completely independent and self-governing and operates democratically under Christ's rule. Each member has equal rights and responsibilities. We are ruled over by no boards, committees, or conventions. Christ alone is our head.

We have no affiliation with the World Council of Churches or any such organization. No one speaks for us, dictates to us, or rules over us. We are completely free and independent.

All matters of business are brought before the congregation as a whole at a regular business meeting, openly discussed, and then voted upon. Each member has one vote and no person has any power except the power of influence. The majority vote rules.

The church has only two officers. They are the pastor or leader, called bishop, elder, and pastor in the New Testament; and the deacon, special servant (Phil. 1:1). When the church needs a pastor, a special committee is elected by the congregation to seek one. They visit and talk with whomsoever they will. Then they find the person they feel God wants them to have. That person is usually then invited to preach before the congregation, and it then votes to approve or disapprove. The pastor remains as long as both he and the congregation feel it is God's will. Deacons are elected from the church membership by vote of the congregation.

2. *The church is spiritual in its mission.* It is our duty as a church to spread the message of Christ to the ends of the earth, to educate in religion, and to do benevolent work. It is the pillar and support of the truth (1 Tim. 3:15). We have learned we can best do this through cooperation with other Baptist churches. Therefore, we have voluntarily organized ourselves into a convention for the purpose of cooperation in achieving these objectives. This association is purely voluntary and the Convention has absolutely no authority over the church. This is the pattern followed by New Testament churches (Acts 15, Gal. 2, 1 Cor. 16:1-2, and 2 Cor. 8—9).

3. *The church is like a family in nature* (1 Tim. 3:15). It is not a building or an organization but a family of God's people. It is composed of those who have entered God's family by becoming a new person by following Christ (new birth) (John 1:12-13; 3:3). It is a place where brothers and sisters in Christ can be helped and brought into spiritual maturity through worship, prayer, study, fellowship, and encouragement (Acts 2:42-47).

In God's family, like most families, we will find people of all ages and all levels of maturity. People are not rejected or condemned because they don't measure up to a certain standard. Families don't do that. Each person is nurtured, loved, and encouraged to become a mature child of the Father.

Some people don't understand that and so they condemn the church because its members aren't perfect. The church is not a place for perfect people to go any more than a hospital is a place for whole people to go. As the hospital is for the sick, so the church is for sinners who fall short of God's ideal, but need and want help. It is not a graduate school for super saints. It is a kindergarten for sinners. There you can find love, acceptance, encouragement, and teaching to help you grow to spiritual maturity. In order to grow, we need all that (1 Pet. 2:2; Heb. 10:25).

Church attendance is vital to every Christian. Those who neglect it do so in violation of the clear command of God and to their own spiritual detriment (Heb. 10:25). We do not go to church to score points with God. He does not check the roll every Sunday to see if we are there. There will be no perfect attendance awards in heaven. We go to church for what we get out of it—teaching, inspiration, encouragement, and nurture in living for Christ.

The church is a local fellowship of God's people who, in love for one another, meet for the common purpose of worship, service, and encouragement. We stand on that!

VI. We Stand on the Stewardship of Life

We believe that God is the source of all blessings both material and spiritual. All we have and are are due to him. Christians owe a spiritual debt to the whole world. We are but trustees of our possessions. We are therefore under obligation to serve him with our time, talents, and material possessions. We should recognize all of these as entrusted to us to be used for the glory of God and we should contribute of our means cheerfully, regularly, and systematically to God's causes around the world (1 Cor. 16:1-2; 2 Cor. 9:6-10; Acts 20:35).

Our churches are supported totally by the freewill offerings of our people. We consider giving a wonderful privilege as well as a sacred duty; for as we support God's work financially, we become fellow-helpers or allies in the truth of God's word. There are no dues or membership assessments in our church. We simply encourage and trust our people to give as God has blessed them.

"The earth is the Lord's and the fulness thereof; the world, and they that dwell therein" (Ps. 24:1). All we have is a trust from him to be used in his service. We stand on that!

VII. We Stand on the Necessity of Christian Living

Christians should live their lives in loving obedience to Christ (John 14:15). This involves more than prayer, Bible study, and worship. It involves both right living and practical goodness.

While we aren't saved by being good or by doing good works, God does expect our lives to be characterized by goodness. This is his purpose in both creation and redemption (Eph. 2:8-10). Jesus went about doing good and so should we (Acts 10:38). We are to do good to all people at every opportunity (Gal. 6:10), with great enthusiasm (Titus 2:14), and without ceasing (Gal. 6:9). He also lived in perfect obedience to God's will (John 4:34), and so should we (Rom. 12:1-2).

Christian living begins when we become new people through faith in Christ (John 3:1-14; 2 Cor. 5:17). From there we grow into the full likeness of Christ in our relationship to both God and men (Eph. 4:13).

All Christians are under obligation to seek to make the teachings of Christ supreme in their own lives, to win the lost to faith in Christ, and to work for the social good of all men.

The believer's life should be characterized by such virtues as love, joy, peace, longsuffering, gentleness, goodness, faith, meekness, and temperance (Gal. 5:22). Believers should oppose in the spirit of Christ every form of greed, selfishness, exploitation, vice, impurity, hate, and dishonesty (Gal. 5:19-20). They should work to provide for the poor, the orphans, the needy, the aged, the sick, the helpless (Jas. 1:27; Matt. 25:34-40). And they should bring the principles of Christ to bear on government, industry, the home, and all of society as they have opportunity (Matt. 23:23 and 1 Cor. 7:23-24).

The church plays a vital part in Christian living. It provides both the stimulus and the primary avenue for its expression. In cooperation with other Christians we can do so much more than we can do alone. And through the church we get encouragement we could not get any other way. Anyone who takes Christian living seriously will take the church seriously also.

So vital is such Christian living that we can question the claims of people who do not live for Christ in their daily lives (Matt. 7:16-20; 1 John 1:7-9). A genuine Christian experience will result in a Christlike character and good works.

Christian living is the natural outgrowth of following Christ. We stand on that!

VIII. We Stand on the Security of the Believer

Becoming a Christian doesn't mean that a person becomes perfect. Being a follower of Christ does not keep a person from temptation or sin. Christians do sin. If people say otherwise, they deceive themselves and contradict God (1 John 1:8-10).

However, real Christians will not knowingly or purposely continue to live in sin. They will confess and repent of their disobedience to God. All true believers endure to the end. Those who have accepted Christ may fall into sin through neglect and temptation and thereby grieve the Holy Spirit, bring reproach on the name of Christ, and even punishment on themselves, yet they will be kept by the power of God through faith unto salvation (2 Tim. 1:12; Jude 24-25; John 10:17-29).

Since we don't earn our salvation by being good, we don't lose it by being bad. Our salvation depends on God's love, power, and forgiveness from start to finish. He keeps us secure.

The Christian life is a life of faith, endurance, and assurance. We stand on that!

This, of course, is not all we stand for. We hold other great truths in common with various religious bodies. Some of these are (1) the existence of God, (2) the deity of Christ, (3) the Trinity, (4) the fall of humanity, (5) the atonement, (6) the immortality of the soul, (7) the resurrection of the dead, and (8) personal accountability to our Maker.

IX. How to Join a Baptist Church

How does a person join a Baptist church? The mechanics are simple, once a heart decision is made. You simply come forward during the invitation (the hymn at the end of the sermon) and tell the pastor of your desire to join the church. He handles the matter completely from there.

You may join a Baptist church in one of four ways:

1. By profession of faith. You come this way if you have recently accepted Christ. Christ has become the ruler of your life, the one who has forgiven your sin and has made you right with God. You confess that fact and follow him in baptism (Rom. 10:9-10; Matt. 10:32-33).

2. By baptism. You come this way if you are already a Christian but a member of another denomination.

3. By letter. You come this way if you are a member of another Baptist church. We write the other church and tell them of your transfer.

4. By statement. You come this way if you have once been a Baptist and transferred to another denomination or if your Baptist membership records have been lost.

When Martin Luther, father of the Reformation, was accused of heresy and the Pope demanded that he recant, Luther took the position that he could not recant while he believed, on the basis of the Scriptures and "evident reason," that he was speaking the truth. Then he said, "Here I stand, I cannot do otherwise. God help me. Amen."

Here we stand. We can do no other. Come stand with us and together we shall move the world for God.